THE
MILITARY
QUOTATION
BOOK

OTHER QUOTATION BOOKS COMPILED AND
EDITED BY JAMES CHARLTON

The Executive's Quotation Book, Revised and Expanded

The Executive's Quotation Book

The Writer's Quotation Book

Legal Briefs

A Little Learning is a Dangerous Thing

On the Night the Hogs Ate Willy (with Barbara Binswanger)

Fighting Words

Book Love (with Bill Henderson)

THE
MILITARY
QUOTATION
BOOK

REVISED FOR THE 21ST CENTURY

More Than 1,100 of the Best Quotations
About War, Leadership, Courage,
and Victory

EDITED BY
James Charlton

THOMAS DUNNE BOOKS
St. Martin's Press ⚉ New York

THOMAS DUNNE BOOKS.
An imprint of St. Martin's Press.

www.thomasdunnebooks.com
www.stmartins.com

Library of Congress Cataloging-in-Publication Data

The military quotation book, revised for the 21st century : more than 1,100 of the best quotations about war, leadership, courage, and victory/edited by James Charlton.—First edition.
    p. cm.
  ISBN 978-1-250-00450-5 (hardcover)
  ISBN 978-1-4668-3472-9 (e-book)
  1. War—Quotations, maxims, etc. 2. Military art and science—Quotations, maxims, etc. I. Charlton, James, 1939–
  U102.M598 2013
  355—dc23

2013003727

First Edition: May 2013

10 9 8 7 6 5 4 3 2 1

THE
MILITARY
QUOTATION
BOOK

INTRODUCTION

This book is about war. War in all its manifestations and effects: the rattling sabers, the feverish preparations, the battles on land, in the air, and at sea, and the feelings at home. This book is also about patriotism and heroism and sacrifice, the vanquished and the victorious. And I hope, finally, that this is a book of inspiration.

The first edition of this book came out in 1990. The second edition came out in 2002. Readers familiar with the lag time between the delivery of a manuscript and its publication can match those dates up with the conflicts and issues not addressed in those volumes; the Gulf War in the initial book; and, in the second volume, 9/11 and the Iraq and Afghanistan conflicts that followed. And now, roughly a decade later, this is the third edition of *The Military Quotation Book,* and we can include quotations from those events.

To be at war, no matter where one is serving, is to sense palpably the possibility of death; if not to you, then to a friend or relative. Many of the quotes included within reflect that omnipresent feeling. British poet Wilfred Owen, a frontline commander in World War I, complimented one of his men with, "Well done. You are doing that very well, my boy."

These were his last words. A number of "last words" on the battlefield I found to be very affecting are preserved in the last chapter of the book. Wilfred Owen died in 1918, but his poetry lives on, as in these lines from "Anthem for a Doomed Youth;"

> What passing-bells for these who die as cattle?
> Only the monstrous anger of the guns.
> Only the stuttering rifles' rapid rattle
> Can patter out their hasty orisons.

Every war has its pacifists, those who are against violence no matter what the cause; often these are people who have not served in the armed forces. But there is another rank of pacifists, a more knowing, and, to my mind, more persuasive type—those who have seen the face of war up close and are horrified by it. Often these are ex-officers, like Dwight Eisenhower, underrated as a commander and as a president, who sounded many warnings about the dangers of war and military preparation. Several of his most eloquent criticisms and statements are in this book. The face of war has changed, and for the first time I have included chapters devoted to the topic of gays and women in the armed forces. The number of quotes on terrorism is, alas, much longer, given the state of our world today.

But no matter what new quotations emerge in the next ten years, the subject of war will always raise passions and emotions. As a writer and editor, I have collected and edited six books of quotations; when I was an editor in chief of a publishing house, I published more than a dozen books of quotations, ranging from sports to music to cooking. None of those books of course aroused the level of feelings reflected in this collection.

This volume is by no means all-inclusive. Encyclopedic works certainly have their place on the library shelves, but to my way of thinking, a carefully selected anthology is preferable. A shorter book of quotations must take a position; the editor must select and edit, rather than merely gather as many sayings as possible. Having said that, this revision of the book is nearly double the size of the first volume published more than two decades ago in part reflecting the changes and events of those years.

I feel a collection of quotations should be a book to read and to browse through, a volume to inspire, amuse, and engage the reader. To be useful, a quotation must reflect a point of view, even if it's one that the reader opposes. It must have been said by an authority or someone well-known. A wonderfully pithy statement made by your sister is just that; the same line uttered by a prime minister, even if penned by a speech writer, is remembered. And quoted. So it is in this book. Military leaders are no different from others when it comes to appropriating a good line for their own. When there was a conflict on authorship—and there often was—I used the more accepted source.

I have tried to include only quotations from individuals whom any well-read lay person would have heard of. There are some exceptions; either the quote was unique or outstanding or fit the situation perfectly, or the person quoted was a military officer with whom a military reader would be familiar.

Many people helped with this book, both with the first and second editions and with this revised volume. These include Major Christopher Kolenda, from the history department at West Point, and the estimable Colonel Phil Meilinger, at the Naval War College. To them, grateful thanks. I want to thank Captain Gil Diaz, who was with the history department of the United States Naval Academy when this project began in 1990. My grateful thanks to the editors at St. Martin's Press: Barbara Anderson, who was the editor on the first volume; the veteran Ruth Cavin, who edited the second book; and the patient and thorough Kat Brzozowski, the editor of this volume. And finally, many thanks to my friend Tom Dunne, publisher at St. Martin's Press, who has been constantly supportive of this book for more than two decades.

Jim Charlton
New York City, August 2012

❦ WARS AND WHY THEY START ❧

There never is a convenient place to fight a war when the other man starts it.

ADMIRAL ARLEIGH A. BURKE

Stand your ground. Don't fire unless fired upon, but if they mean to have a war, let it begin here!

JOHN PARKER

Although war is evil, it is occasionally the lesser of two evils.

MCGEORGE BUNDY

It is far easier to make war than to make peace.

GEORGES CLEMENCEAU

War will exist until that distant day when the conscientious objector enjoys the same reputation and prestige that the warrior does today.

JOHN F. KENNEDY

The tendency to aggression is an innate, independent, instinctual disposition in man . . . it constitutes the most powerful obstacle to culture.

SIGMUND FREUD

War will never cease until babies begin to come into the world with larger cerebrums and smaller adrenal glands.

H. L. MENCKEN

War is a biological necessity.

FRIEDRICH A. J. VON BERNHARDI, German cavalry general

War is life multiplied by some number that no one has ever heard of.

SEBASTIAN JUNGER, *War*

War is to man what maternity is to a woman. From a philosophical and doctrinal viewpoint, I do not believe in perpetual peace.

BENITO MUSSOLINI

Most sorts of diversion in men, children and other animals, are in imitation of fighting.

JONATHAN SWIFT

Most quarrels are inevitable at the time; incredible afterwards.

E. M. FORSTER

℞ CAUSES OF WAR ℠

Wars frequently begin ten years before the first shot is fired.
MAJOR K. K. V. CASEY

We all muddled into war.
DAVID LLOYD GEORGE

Wars spring from unseen and generally insignificant causes, the first outbreak being often but an explosion of anger.
THUCYDIDES

I used to think that the causes of war were predominantly economic. I came to think that they were more psychological. I am now coming to think that they are decisively "personal," arising from the defects and ambitions of those who have the power to influence the currents of nations.
B. H. LIDDELL HART

It is simply not true that war is solely a means to an end, nor do people necessarily fight in order to obtain this objective or that. In fact, the opposite is true: people very often take up one objective or another precisely in order that they may fight.
MARTIN VAN CREVELD, Israeli military historian

But that was war. Just about all he could find in its favor was that it paid well and liberated children from the pernicious influence of their parents.

JOSEPH HELLER, *Catch-22*

❧ WILL TO WIN ❧

It is fatal to enter any war without the will to win it.

GENERAL DOUGLAS MACARTHUR

If you start to take Vienna—take Vienna.

NAPOLEON BONAPARTE

The power to wage war is the power to wage war successfully.

CHIEF JUSTICE CHARLES EVANS HUGHES

Whoever conquers a free town and does not demolish it commits a great error and may expect to be ruined himself.

NICCOLO MACHIAVELLI

You don't hurt 'em if you don't hit 'em.

LIEUTENANT GENERAL LEWIS "CHESTY" PULLER

Treating your adversary with respect is striking soft in battle.

SAMUEL JOHNSON

◈ PREPARATION ◈

Preparation for war is a constant stimulus to suspicion and ill will.

JAMES MONROE

We have never been likely to get into trouble by having an extra thousand or two up-to-date airplanes at our disposal. As the man whose mother-in-law had died in Brazil replied, when asked how the remains should be disposed of, "Embalm, cremate, bury. Take no risks."

WINSTON CHURCHILL

In preparing for battle I have always found that plans are useless, but planning is indispensable.

GENERAL DWIGHT D. EISENHOWER

Prepare for the unknown by studying how others in the past have coped with the unforeseeable and the unpredictable.

GENERAL GEORGE S. PATTON

If I always appear prepared, it is because before entering an undertaking, I have meditated long and have foreseen what might occur. It is not genius which reveals to me suddenly and secretly what I should do in circumstances unexpected by others; it is thought and preparation.

NAPOLEON BONAPARTE

As a nation we were not prepared for World War II. Yes, we won the war, but at a terrific cost in lives, human suffering, and material, and at times the margin was narrow. History alone can reveal how many turning points there were, how many times we were near losing, and how our enemies' mistakes often pulled us through. In the flush of victory, some like to forget unpalatable truths.

GENERAL HENRY "HAP" ARNOLD

If we should have to fight, we should be prepared to do so from the neck up instead of from the neck down.

GENERAL JIMMY DOOLITTLE

❦ MILITARY TRAINING ❧

The aim of military training is not just to prepare men for battle, but to make them long for it.

LOUIS SIMPSON, *North to Jamaica*

The instruments of battle are valuable only if one knows how to use them.

ARDANT DU PICQ, *Battle Studies*

Never give a sword to a man who can't dance.

Celtic motto

To lead an untrained people to war is to throw them away.

CONFUCIUS

A handful of men, inured to war, proceed to certain victory, while on the contrary, numerous armies of raw and undisciplined troops are but multitudes of men dragged to the slaughter.

VEGETIUS

If, in order to succeed in an enterprise, I were obliged to choose between fifty deer commanded by a lion, and fifty lions commanded by a deer, I should consider myself more certain of success with the first group than with the second.

SAINT VINCENT DE PAUL

Ten soldiers wisely led will beat a hundred without a head.

EURIPIDES

◌ GOOD WAR/BAD WAR ◌

There is hardly such a thing as a war in which it makes no difference who wins. Nearly always one side stands more or less for progress, the other side more or less for reaction.

GEORGE ORWELL

There is such a thing as legitimate warfare: war has its laws; there are things which may fairly be done, and things which may not be done.

JOHN HENRY CARDINAL NEWMAN

What difference does it make to the dead, the orphans, and the homeless, whether the mad destruction is wrought under the name of totalitarianism or the holy name of liberty or democracy?

MAHATMA GANDHI

What the hell difference does it make, left or right? There were good men lost on both sides.

BRENDAN BEHAN

The wrong war, at the wrong place, at the wrong time, and with the wrong enemy.

GENERAL OMAR BRADLEY, on the proposal to carry the Korean conflict into China

Within the soul of each Vietnam veteran there is probably something that says, "bad war, good soldier."

MAX CLELAND

To those for whom war is necessary, it is just; and resort to arms is righteous for those to whom no further hope remains.

LIVY

ଔ BRAVERY ଵ

It sometimes helps if you sort out in your mind the very real difference between being brave and being fearless. Being brave means doing or facing something frightening. . . . Being fearless means being without fear.

PENELOPE LEACH

Bravery is the capacity to perform properly even when scared half to death.

GENERAL OMAR BRADLEY

I don't know what effect these men will have on the enemy, but, by God, they frighten me.

ARTHUR WELLESLEY, Duke of Wellington, on replacements sent to him in Spain

The Guard dies; it does not surrender.

GENERAL PIERRE CAMBRONNE, of the Imperial Guard at Waterloo

Brave rifles, veterans, you have been baptized in fire and blood and have come out steel!

GENERAL WINFIELD SCOTT, 1812

All I ask of fate is that I may be killed leading a cavalry charge.

MAJOR GENERAL JEB STUART, killed in a charge at Yellow Tavern, 1864

The bravest are surely those who have the clearest vision of what is before them, glory and danger alike, and yet notwithstanding go out to meet it.

THUCYDIDES

Valor lies just halfway between rashness and cowardice.

MIGUEL DE CERVANTES

Only the brave know how to forgive. . . . A coward never forgave; it is not in his nature.

LAURENCE STERNE

It is thus that mutual cowardice keeps us in peace. Were one half of mankind brave and one cowards, the brave would be always beating the cowards. Were all brave, they would lead a very uneasy life; all would be continually fighting; but being all cowards, we go on very well.

SAMUEL JOHNSON

The world is in a constant conspiracy against the brave. It's the age-old struggle—the roar of the crowd on the one side— and the voice of your conscience on the other.

GENERAL DOUGLAS MACARTHUR

❦ COURAGE ❧

Rascals! Would you live forever?

FREDERICK THE GREAT, leading reluctant soldiers into battle

Come on, you sons of bitches—do you want to live forever?
GUNNERY SERGEANT DANIEL DALY, USMC, near Lucy-le-Bocage, June 6, 1918

Cowards die many times before their death; the valiant never taste of death but once.
WILLIAM SHAKESPEARE, *Julius Caesar*

Two qualities are indispensable: first, an intellect that, even in the darkest hour, retains some glimmerings of the inner light which leads to truth; and second, the courage to follow this faint light wherever it may lead.
CARL VON CLAUSEWITZ

Cowardice . . . is almost always simply a lack of ability to suspend the functioning of the imagination.
ERNEST HEMINGWAY

Courage is rightly esteemed the first of human qualities . . . because it is the quality which guarantees all others.
WINSTON CHURCHILL

The first virtue in a soldier is endurance of fatigue; courage is only the second virtue.
NAPOLEON BONAPARTE

Moral courage is higher and a rarer virtue than physical courage.

FIELD MARSHAL SIR WILLIAM J. SLIM

One man with courage is a majority.

THOMAS JEFFERSON

It is not because things are difficult that we do not dare; it is because we do not dare that they are difficult.

SENECA

War is fear cloaked in courage.

GENERAL WILLIAM WESTMORELAND

One man with courage makes a majority.

ANDREW JACKSON

The courage we desire and prize is not the courage to die decently, but to live manfully.

THOMAS CARLYLE

Courage is resistance to fear, mastery of fear, not absence of fear.

MARK TWAIN

Courage is the fear of being thought a coward.

HORACE SMITH

Courage is fear holding on a minute longer.

GENERAL GEORGE S. PATTON

But I firmly believe that any man's finest hour, his greatest fulfillment of all he holds dear, is the moment when he has worked his heart out in a good cause and lies exhausted on the field of battle—victorious.

VINCE LOMBARDI

Courtesy is as much a mark of a gentleman as courage.

THEODORE ROOSEVELT

Courage is the price that Life exacts for granting peace.

AMELIA EARHART

❦ HEROES ❧

In war the heroes always outnumber the soldiers ten to one.

H. L. MENCKEN

Show me a hero, and I'll show you a bum.

MAJOR GREG "PAPPY" BOYINGTON

It doesn't take a hero to order men into battle. It takes a hero to be one of those men who goes into battle.

GENERAL NORMAN SCHWARTZKOPF

Unhappy the land that is in need of heroes.

BERTOLT BRECHT

A hero is no braver than an ordinary man, but he is brave five minutes longer.

RALPH WALDO EMERSON

The ordinary man is involved in action, the hero acts. An immense difference.

HENRY MILLER

I'm no hero. Heroes are for the late show.

SARGEANT PHILLIP ARTEBURY. His letter containing the quote is etched in glass and anchors the Vietnam Memorial in Washington DC.

This thing of being a hero, about the main thing to it is to know when to die.

WILL ROGERS

Now I want you to remember that no bastard won a war by dying for his country. He won it by making the other poor dumb bastard die for his country.

GENERAL GEORGE S. PATTON

No hero is mortal till he dies.

W. H. AUDEN

It's not that I'm afraid to die. I just don't want to be there when it happens.

WOODY ALLEN

Although prepared for martyrdom, I preferred that it be post poned.

WINSTON CHURCHILL

Being a hero is the shortest-lived profession on earth.

WILL ROGERS

Show me a hero and I'll write you a tragedy.

F. SCOTT FITZGERALD

And each man stands with his face in the light
Of his own drawn sword,
Ready to do what a hero can.

ELIZABETH BARRETT BROWNING

Fighting is like champagne. It goes to the heads of cowards as quickly as of heroes. Any fool can be brave on a battlefield when it's be brave or else be killed.

MARGARET MITCHELL

A man who is not afraid is not aggressive, a man who has no sense of fear of any kind is really a free, a peaceful man.

JIDDU KRISHNAMURTI

Never in the field of human conflict was so much owed by so many to so few.

WINSTON CHURCHILL, on British airmen in the Battle of Britain

All men who value life more than the glory of the nation and the esteem of their comrades should not be members of the French army.

NAPOLEON BONAPARTE

Glory is being shot at and having your name misspelled in the papers.

MAJOR GENERAL OLIVER O. HOWARD

The paradox of courage is that a man must be a little careless of his life even in order to keep it.

G. K. CHESTERTON

◌ PERSEVERANCE ◌

It is a fact that under equal conditions, large-scale battles and whole wars are won by troops which have a strong will for victory, clear goals before them, high moral standards and devotion to the banner under which they go into battle.

RUSSIAN GENERAL GEORGY ZHUKOV

Let us therefore brace ourselves to our duty and so bear ourselves that if the British Empire and its Commonwealth lasts for a thousand years men will still say, "This was their finest hour."

WINSTON CHURCHILL

War is the domain of physical exertion and suffering.

CARL VON CLAUSEWITZ

In a man to man fight, the winner is he who has one more round in his magazine.

FIELD MARSHAL ERWIN ROMMEL

In every battle there comes a time when both sides consider themselves beaten, then he who continues the attack wins.

GENERAL ULYSSES S. GRANT

There are no secrets to success: Don't waste your time looking for them. Success is the result of perfection, hard work, learning from failure, loyalty to those for whom you work, and persistence.

GENERAL COLIN POWELL

I don't measure a man's success by how high he climbs but how high he bounces when he hits bottom.

GENERAL GEORGE S. PATTON

What counts is not necessarily the size of the dog in the fight, it's the size of the fight in the dog.

GENERAL DWIGHT D. EISENHOWER

It is not the big armies that win battles; it is the good ones.

MARSHAL MAURICE DE SAXE

We will either find a way or make one.

HANNIBAL

❧ FEAR ❧

A revealing light is thrown on this subject through the studies by Medical Corps psychiatrists of the combat fatigue cases in the European Theater. They found that fear of killing, rather than fear of being killed, was the most common cause of battle failure, and that fear of failure ran a strong second.

S. L. A. MARSHALL

My aim, then, was to whip the rebels, to humble their pride, to follow them to their inmost recesses, and make them fear and dread us. Fear is the beginning of wisdom.

GENERAL WILLIAM T. SHERMAN

Battle is the most magnificent competition in which a human being can indulge. It brings out all that is best; it removes all that is base. All men are afraid in battle. The coward is the one who lets his fear overcome his sense of duty. Duty is the essence of manhood.

GENERAL GEORGE S. PATTON

Discipline strengthens the mind so that it becomes impervious to the corroding influence of fear.

FIELD MARSHAL BERNARD MONTGOMERY

He who is afraid is half beaten.

FIELD MARSHAL ALEKSANDR SUVOROV

∞ DUTY, HONOR, COUNTRY ∞

Do your duty in all things. You cannot do more, you should never wish to do less.

GENERAL ROBERT E. LEE

It was duty, honor, country . . . our country had been attacked. . . . It was freedom vs. oppression. It was against imperialism and against fascism, and the country was so together, and I wanted to be on the cutting edge.

GEORGE H. W. BUSH, on his decision to enlist in 1941

To do their duty is their only holiday, and they deem the quiet of inaction to be as disagreeable as the most tiresome business.

THUCYDIDES, *History of the Peloponnesian War*, on the Athenians

Theirs not to make reply,
Theirs not to reason why,
Theirs but to do and die:
Into the Valley of Death

Rode the six hundred.

ALFRED, LORD TENNYSON, "The Charge of the Light Brigade"

You have a mission of sacrifice; here is a post of honor where they want to attack. Every day you will have casualties, because they will disturb your work. On the day they want to, they will massacre you to the last man, and it is your duty to fall.

LIEUTENANT RAYMOND JURBERT, instructions to his men at Verdun, 1916

Duty is the most sublime word in the English language.

GENERAL ROBERT E. LEE

When a stupid man is doing something he is ashamed of, he always declares that it is his duty.

GEORGE BERNARD SHAW

Our honor lies in doing our duty toward our people and our own fatherland, as well as in the consciousness of our mutual obligation to keep faith with one another, so we can depend on each other. We must remember that, even in our technological age, it is man's fighting spirit that ultimately decides between victory and defeat.

BARON HASSO VON MANTEUFFEL

Better to fight for something than live for nothing.

GENERAL GEORGE S. PATTON

It is better to die on your feet than to live on your knees.

EMILIANO ZAPATA

These are the times that try men's souls. The summer soldier and the sunshine patriot will, in this crisis, shrink from the service of their country; but he that stands now, deserves the love and thanks of man and woman.

THOMAS PAINE

It is a fearful thing to lead this great peaceful people into war, into the most terrible and disastrous of all wars, civilization itself seeming to be in the balance. But the right is more precious than peace, and we shall fight for the things which we have always carried nearest our hearts—for democracy.

WOODROW WILSON

I only regret that I have but one life to lose for my country.

NATHAN HALE

If a country is worth living in, it is worth fighting for.

MANNING COLES

Patriotism is easy to understand in America. It means looking out for yourself by looking out for your country.

CALVIN COOLIDGE

When I am abroad, I always make it a rule never to criticize or attack the government of my own country. I make up for lost time when I come home.

WINSTON CHURCHILL

Ask not what your country can do for you—ask what you can do for your country.

JOHN F. KENNEDY

Our country! In her intercourse with foreign nations, may she always be in the right; but our country, right or wrong.

STEPHEN DECATUR

"My country right or wrong" is like saying, "My mother drunk or sober."

G. K. CHESTERTON

A man may devote himself to death and destruction to save a nation; but no nation will devote itself to death and destruction to save mankind.

SAMUEL TAYLOR COLERIDGE

Let every nation know, whether it wishes us well or ill, that we shall pay any price, bear any burden, meet any hardship, support any friend, oppose any foe, in order to assure the survival and the success of liberty.

JOHN F. KENNEDY

This will remain the land of the free only so long as it is the home of the brave.

ELMER DAVIS

⚘ PATRIOTISM ⚘

Each man must for himself alone decide what is right and what is wrong, which course is patriotic and which isn't. You cannot shirk this and be a man. To decide against your conviction is to be an unqualified and inexcusable traitor, both to yourself and to your country, let men label you as they may.

MARK TWAIN

Patriotism has served, at different times, as widely different ends as a razor, which ought to be used in keeping your face clean and yet may be used to cut your own throat or that of an innocent person.

C. E. MONTAGUE

Patriotism is not enough, I must have no hatred or bitterness to anyone.

EDITH CAVELL, a British nurse in WWI, executed by the Germans for helping Allied servicemen escape

You're not supposed to be so blind with patriotism that you can't face reality. Wrong is wrong no matter who does it or who says it.

MALCOM X

Patriotism is your conviction that this country is superior to all other countries because you were born in it.

GEORGE BERNARD SHAW

The man who loves other countries as much as his own stands on a level with the man who loves other women as much as he loves his own wife.

THEODORE ROOSEVELT

Nationalism is an infantile disease. It is the measles of mankind.

ALBERT EINSTEIN

Patriotism is a kind of religion; it is the egg from which wars are hatched.

GUY DE MAUPASSANT

Patriotism is the willingness to kill and be killed for trivial reasons.

BERTRAND RUSSELL

A thing is not necessarily true because a man dies for it.

OSCAR WILDE

Patriotism is the last refuge of a scoundrel.

SAMUEL JOHNSON

Not for the flag
Of any land because myself was born there
Will I give up my life.
But I will love that land where man is free,
And that will I defend.

EDNA ST. VINCENT MILLAY, "Not for a Nation"

What this country needs—what every country needs occasionally—is a good hard bloody war to revive the vice of patriotism on which its existence as a nation depends.

AMBROSE BIERCE

ᑫ CHARACTER ᑢ

That's the whole challenge of life—to act with honor and
hope and generosity, no matter what you've drawn. You can't
help when or what you were born, you may not be able to help
how you die; but you can—and you should—try to pass the
days between as a good man.

ANTON MYRER, *Once an Eagle*

A man of character in peace is a man of courage in war.

CHARLES WILSON, First Baron Moran

Strength of character and inner fortitude, however, are decisive factors. The confidence of the man in the ranks rests upon
a man's strength of character.

ERICH VON MANSTEIN

The first and last essential of an efficient soldier is character; without it he will not long endure the perils of modern war.

CHARLES WILSON, First Baron Moran

It is soldiers who pay most of the human cost. In war it is extraordinary how it all comes down to the character of one man.

GENERAL CREIGHTON W. ABRAMS

Few men during their lifetime come anywhere near exhausting the resources dwelling within them. There are deep wells of strength that are never used.

ADMIRAL RICHARD BYRD

There are only two powers in the world. . . . The sword and the spirit. In the long run, the sword is always defeated by the spirit.

NAPOLEON BONAPARTE

War is no longer a series of battles, but a test of strength of the entire nation, its moral strength as well as physical, brain as well as muscles, and stamina as well as courage.

MARSHAL OF THE RAF SIR ARTHUR TEDDER

In war, moral considerations make up three-quarters of the game: the relative balance of manpower accounts only for the remaining quarter.

NAPOLEON BONAPARTE

⪥ FREEDOM ⪤

If a nation values anything more than freedom, it will lose that freedom; and the irony of it is that if it is comfort or money that it values more, it will lose that, too.

W. SOMERSET MAUGHAM

A people that values its privileges above its principles soon loses both.

DWIGHT D. EISENHOWER

Liberty means responsibility. That is why most men dread it.

GEORGE BERNARD SHAW

One should never put on one's best trousers to go out to battle for freedom and truth.

HENRIK IBSEN

The enemies of freedom do not argue; they shout and they shoot.

WILLIAM RALPH INGE

Do these people even want us here? Can you find anyone to thank us for giving them democracy and freedom?

GEORGE W. BUSH, to General John Abizaid

Man was born free and everywhere he is in shackles.

JEAN-JACQUES ROUSSEAU

The lamps are going out all over Europe; we shall not see them lit again in our lifetime.

SIR EDWARD GREY, on the eve of World War I

You can't separate peace from freedom because no one can be at peace unless he has his freedom.

MALCOM X

Ꮭ NATURE OF BATTLE Ꮮ

War is not an affair of chance. A great deal of knowledge, study, and meditation is necessary to conduct it well.

FREDERICK THE GREAT

Every action is seen to fall into one of three main categories, guarding, hitting, or moving. Here, then, are the elements of combat, whether in war or pugilism.

B. H. LIDDELL HART

There is no "battle line" in modern war. There are battle areas and volumes, which must nowadays be regarded as being as mobile as the forces within them.

AIR MARSHAL E. LUDLOW-HEWITT, 1937

Let us never forget this: since the day of the air, the old frontiers are gone. When you think of the defence of England you no longer think of the chalk cliffs of Dover; you think of the Rhine. That is where our frontier lies.

STANLEY BALDWIN, British Prime Minister, 1934

You don't fight this fellow rifle to rifle. You locate him and back away. Blow the hell out of him and then police up.

BRIGADIER GENERAL GLENN D. WALKER, 1965

For the first time in my life I have seen "History" at close quarters, and I know that its actual process is very different from what is presented to posterity.

GENERAL MAX HOFFMAN, WWI diary entry

It is absolutely true in war, were other things equal, that numbers, whether men, shells, bombs, etc., would be supreme. Yet it is also absolutely true that other things are never equal and can never be equal.

MAJOR GENERAL J. F. C. FULLER

I tell you how it should all be done. Whenever there's a big war coming, you should rope off a big field and sell tickets. And, on the big day, you should take all the kings and cabinets and their generals, put them in the center dressed in their underpants and let them fight it out with clubs.

LOUIS WOLHEIM, as Katczinsky in *All Quiet on the Western Front*

Generals think war should be waged like the tourneys of the Middle Ages. I have no use for knights; I need revolutionaries.

ADOLF HITLER

Loss of hope rather than loss of life is what decides the issues of war. But helplessness induces hopelessness.

B. H. LIDDELL HART

☙ COMBAT ❧

I hate war as only a soldier who has lived it can, only as one who has seen its brutality, its futility, its stupidity.

DWIGHT D. EISENHOWER

I think I'd be a better president because I was in combat.

GEORGE H. W. BUSH

Life has a certain flavor for those who have fought and risked all that the sheltered and protected can never experience.

JOHN STUART MILL

I'm inclined to think that a military background wouldn't hurt anyone.

WILLIAM FAULKNER

One crowded hour of glorious life is worth an age without a name.

SIR WALTER SCOTT

Don't fire until you see the whites of their eyes.

COLONEL WILLIAM PRESCOTT, Revolutionary War

Elevate those guns a little lower.

ANDREW JACKSON

On the battlefield, self-discipline plays a much greater role in modern combat than discipline imposed from without.

ANTHONY KELLETT, *Contemporary Studies in Combat Psychology*

War, the ordinary man's most convenient means of escaping from the ordinary.

PHILIP CAPUTO

War makes strange giant creatures out of us little routine men who inhabit the earth.

ERNIE PYLE

War means fighting, and fighting means killing.

NATHAN BEDFORD FORREST

A young man who does not have what it takes to perform military service is not likely to have what it takes to make a living. Today's military rejects include tomorrow's hard core unemployed.

JOHN F. KENNEDY

One knows what a war is about only when it is over.

H. N. BRAILSFORD

When it is over and you're home once more, you can thank God that twenty years from now, when you're sitting around the fireside with your grandson on your knee and he asks what you did in the war, you won't have to shift him to the other knee, cough, and say, "I shoveled shit in Louisiana."

GENERAL GEORGE S. PATTON, to troops before D Day, June 6, 1944

The news couldn't be better. As long as they were in Britain we couldn't get at them. Now we have them where we can destroy them.

ADOLPH HITLER, upon hearing that D Day had started

◎ THE BATTLEFIELD ◎

Battle is an orgy of disorder.

GENERAL GEORGE S. PATTON

Every soldier must know, before he goes into battle, how the little battle he is to fight fits into the larger picture, and how the success of his fighting will influence the battle as a whole.

FIELD MARSHAL BERNARD MONTGOMERY

Man's fate in battle is worked out before the war begins.

CHARLES WILSON, First Baron Moran

I have always regarded the forward edge of the battlefield as the most exclusive club in the world.

SIR BRIAN HORROCKS

There's no such thing as a crowded battlefield. Battlefields are lonely places.

GENERAL ALFRED M. GRAY

The most terrible job in warfare is to be a second lieutenant leading a platoon when you are on the battlefield.

DWIGHT D. EISENHOWER

The battlefield is cold. . . . It is the lonesomest place which men share together.

S. L. A. MARSHALL

Everything is simple in war, but the simplest thing is difficult. These difficulties accumulate and produce a friction which no man can imagine exactly who has not seen war.

CARL VON CLAUSEWITZ

No study is possible on the battlefield.

MARSHAL OF FRANCE FERDINAND FOCH

ℛ CASUALTIES ℘

In a war of ideas it is people who get killed.

STANISŁAW LEC

In reality, it is more fruitful to wound than to kill. While the dead man lies still, counting only one man less, the wounded man is a progressive drain upon his side.

B. H. LIDDELL HART

See that little stream, we could walk to it in two minutes. It took the British a whole month to walk to it, a whole empire walking very slowly, dying in front and pushing forward behind. And another empire walked very slowly backward a few inches a day, leaving the dead like a million bloody rugs.

F. SCOTT FITZGERALD

I was very careful to send Mr. Roosevelt every few days a statement of our casualties. I tried to keep before him all the time the casualty results because you get hardened to these things and you have to be very careful to keep them always in the forefront of your mind.

GENERAL GEORGE MARSHALL

I have given instructions that I be informed every time one of our soldiers is killed, even if it is in the middle of the night. When President Nasser leaves instructions that he is to be awakened in the middle of the night if an Egyptian soldier is killed, there will be peace.

GOLDA MEIR

I'm not saying we wouldn't get our hair mussed, but I do say no more than ten to twenty million killed, tops, depending on the breaks!

GEORGE C. SCOTT, as General "Buck" Turgidson in *Dr. Strangelove or: How I Learned to Stop Worrying and Love the Bomb*

It takes 15,000 casualties to train a major general.

MARSHAL OF FRANCE FERDINAND FOCH

To me an unnecessary action, or shot, or casualty, was not only waste but sin.

T. E. LAWRENCE

War is war. The only good human being is a dead one.

GEORGE ORWELL

Where are your legs that used to run
When ent to carry a gun
Indeed your dancing days are done
Oh Johnny, I hardly knew ye.
Irish folk song "Johnny I Hardly Knew Ye"

❧ CIVILIANS ❧

We come to give you liberty and equality, but don't lose your heads about it; the first person who stirs without permission will be shot.

MARSHAL PIERRE LEFEBRE, upon occupying a Franconian town

Except when war is waged in a desert, noncombatants, also known as civilians or "the people," constitute the great majority of those affected.

MARTIN VAN CREVELD

If civilians are going to be killed, I would rather have them be their civilians than our civilians.

SENATOR STUART SYMINGTON

You've got to forget about this civilian. Whenever you drop bombs, you're going to hit civilians.

SENATOR BARRY GOLDWATER

The only defense is offense, which means that you have to kill more women and children more quickly than the enemy if you wish to save yourselves.

STANLEY BALDWIN

The civilian is a soldier on 11 months annual leave.

ISRAELI GENERAL YIGAEL YADIN

The functions of a citizen and a soldier are inseparable.

BENITO MUSSOLINI

Every citizen [should] be a soldier. This was the case with the Greeks and the Romans, and must be that of every free state.

THOMAS JEFFERSON

It may be laid down as a primary position, and the basis of our system, that every Citizen who enjoys the protection of a Free Government, owes not only a proportion of his property, but even of his personal services to the defense of it.

GEORGE WASHINGTON

✥ AIRPOWER ✥

Send one plane it's a sortie; send two it's a flight; send four and it's a test of airpower.

RICHARD KOHN, 1990

As the aeroplane is the most mobile weapon we possess, it is destined to become the dominant offensive arm of the future.

MAJOR GENERAL J. F. C. FULLER

With us air people, the future of our nation is indissolubly bound up in the development of airpower.

BRIGADIER GENERAL BILLY MITCHELL

Airpower is a thunderbolt launched from an eggshell invisibly tethered to a base.

HOFFMAN NICKERSON

Airpower speaks a strategic language so new that translation into the hackneyed idiom of the past is impossible.

ALEXANDER DE SEVERSKY

Airpower is indivisible. If you split it up into compartments, you merely pull it to pieces and destroy its greatest asset, its flexibility.

FIELD MARSHAL BERNARD MONTGOMERY

Airpower is like poker. A second-best hand is like none at all—it will cost you dough and win you nothing.

GEORGE KENNEY

The advent of airpower, which can go straight to the vital centers and either neutralize or destroy them, has put a completely new complexion on the old system of making war. It is now realized that the hostile main army in the field is a false objective, and the real objectives are the vital centers.

BRIGADIER GENERAL BILLY MITCHELL

Neither the Army nor the Navy is of any protection, or very little protection, against aerial raids.

ALEXANDER GRAHAM BELL

Airpower can either paralyze the enemy's military action or compel him to devote to the defense of his bases and communications a share of his straitened resources far greater than what we need in the attack.

WINSTON CHURCHILL

The future battle on the ground will be preceded by battle in the air. This will determine which of the contestants has to suffer operational and tactical disadvantages and be forced throughout the battle into adopting compromise solutions.

FIELD MARSHAL ERWIN ROMMEL

So long as large armies go to battle, so long will the air arm remain their spearhead.

CYRIL FALLS

Today airpower is the dominant factor in war. It may not win a war by itself alone, but without it no major war can be won.

ADMIRAL ARTHUR RADFORD, 1954

An air force commander must exploit the extreme flexibility, the high tactical mobility, and the supreme offensive quality inherent in air forces, to mystify and mislead his enemy, and so to threaten his various vital centers as to compel him to be dangerously weak at the point which is really decisive at the time.

MARSHAL OF THE RAF SIR JOHN C. SLESSOR

Strange as it may seem, the Air Force, except in the air, is the least mobile of all the Services. A squadron can reach its destination in a few hours, but its establishment, depots, fuel, spare parts, and workshops take many weeks, and even months to develop.

WINSTON CHURCHILL

Airpower is an unusually seductive form of military strength, in part because, like modern courtship, it appears to offer gratification without commitment.

ELIOT COHEN

Offense is the essence of airpower.

GENERAL HENRY "HAP" ARNOLD

☞ AIR SUPERIORITY ☜

Nothing can stop the attack of aircraft except other aircraft.

BRIGADIER GENERAL BILLY MITCHELL

But after all, the great defence against the air menace is to attack the enemy's aircraft as near as possible to their point of departure.

WINSTON CHURCHILL, 1914

If we lose the war in the air we lose the war and we lose it quickly.

FIELD MARSHAL BERNARD MONTGOMERY

To commit troops to a campaign in which they cannot be provided with adequate air support is to court disaster.

FIELD MARSHAL CLAUDE AUCHINLECK, 1940

Anyone who has to fight, even with the most modern weapons, against an enemy in complete command of the air, fights like a savage against modern European troops, under the same handicaps and with the same chances of success.

FIELD MARSHAL ERWIN ROMMEL

The Normandy Invasion was based on a deep-seated faith in the power of the air forces, in overwhelming numbers, to intervene in the land battle . . . Without that air force, without the aid of the enemy air force out of the sky, without its power to intervene in the land battle, that invasion would have been fantastic . . . Unless we had faith in the airpower to intervene and make safe that landing, it would have been more than fantastic, it would have been criminal.

GENERAL DWIGHT D. EISENHOWER, 1945

The first lesson is that you can't lose a war if you have command of the air, and you can't win a war if you haven't.

GENERAL JIMMY DOOLITTLE

If you want to go anywhere in modern war, in the air, on the sea, on the land, you must have command of the air.

ADMIRAL WILLIAM "BULL" HALSEY, JR., 1946

The power of an air force is terrific when there is nothing to oppose it.

WINSTON CHURCHILL

It is far more important to be able to hit the target than it is to haggle over who makes a weapon or who pulls a trigger.

DWIGHT D. EISENHOWER

The third peculiarity of aerial warfare was that it was at once enormously destructive and entirely indecisive.

H. G. WELLS

ℜ AIR BOMBARDMENT ℛ

A country which cannot defend itself from aerial attack will find its air bases, its munitions centres, its military depots, its shipyards, and its great cities subjected to a devastating rain of bombs within a few hours of the declaration of hostilities.

BRIGADIER GENERAL P. R. C. GROVES, RAF, 1922

To me our bombing policy appears to be suicidal. Not because it does not do vast damage to our enemy, it does; but because, simultaneously, it does vast damage to our peace aim, unless that aim is mutual economic and social annihilation.

MAJOR GENERAL J. F. C. FULLER

The Nazis entered this war under the rather childish delusion that they were going to bomb everybody else, and that nobody was going to bomb them. At Rotterdam, London, Warsaw, and half a hundred other places they put that rather naive theory into operation. They sowed the wind, and now they are going to reap the whirlwind.

AIR CHIEF MARSHAL SIR ARTHUR HARRIS, RAF Bomber Command, 1943

Merely on the basis of the B-29s alone I was convinced that Japan should sue for peace. I myself, on the basis of the B-29 raids, felt that the cause was hopeless.

BARON KANTARO ZUZUKI, Premier of Japan, 1945

We never dreamed that airpower could have affected the progress of the war to such an extent.

GENERAL TOSHIGO NISHIO, Governor of Tokyo, 1945

The one effective method of defending one's own territory from an offensive by air is to destroy the enemy's airpower with the greatest possible speed.

ITALIAN GENERAL GIULIO DOUHET

What you're seeing here is an ass-kicking of Biblical proportions.

Sign in Pentagon office during Persian Gulf War, 1991

I am convinced that a bombing attack launched from such carriers [the USS *Lexington* and *Saratoga*] from an unknown point, at an unknown instant, with an unknown objective, cannot be warded off.

ADMIRAL WILLIAM A. MOFFETT, at the christening of the USS *Lexington,* October 3, 1925

❦ DECISIVENESS OF AIRPOWER ❧

The real importance of Munich . . . is that it was the first victory for airpower, no less significant for being temporarily bloodless.

MARSHAL OF THE RAF SIR JOHN C. SLESSOR

For the first time in some 5,000 years of military history, we saw an independent air operation produce a political result.

GENERAL MICHAEL J. DUGAN, on Kosovo, 1999

Iraq went from having the fourth largest army in the world to having the fourth largest army in Iraq.

American pilot during the Persian Gulf War

The day we executed the air campaign, I said, "we gotcha!"

GENERAL NORMAN SCHWARZKOPF

❦ LEADERSHIP ❧

It is highly indicative of good leadership when people obey someone without coercion and are prepared to remain by him during times of danger.

XENOPHON

I cannot approve of your method of operation, you proceed like a bewildered idiot, taking not the least notice of my orders.

NAPOLEON BONAPARTE, to Marshal Murat, 1805

Some men think that modern armies may be so regulated that a general can sit in an office and play his several columns as on the keys of a piano; this is a fearful mistake. The directing mind must be at the very head of the army, must be seen there, the effect of his mind and personal energy must be felt by every officer and man present with it, to secure the best results. Every attempt to make war easy and safe will result in humiliation and disaster.

GENERAL WILLIAM T. SHERMAN

In the World War nothing was more dreadful to witness than a chain of men starting with a battalion commander and ending with an army commander sitting in telephone boxes, improvised or actual, talking, talking, talking, in place of leading, leading, leading.

MAJOR GENERAL J. F. C. FULLER

To understand the nature of the people one must be a prince, and to understand the nature of a prince, one must be of the people.

NICCOLO MACHIAVELLI

Good generals, unlike poets, are made rather than born, and will never reach the first rank without much study of their profession; but they must have certain natural gifts, the power of quick decision, judgment, boldness, and, I am afraid, a considerable degree of toughness, almost callousness, which is harder to find as civilization progresses.

FIELD MARSHAL ARCHIBALD PERCIVAL WAVELL, First Earl Wavell

The leader must aim high, see big, judge widely, thus setting himself apart from the ordinary people who debate in narrow confines.

CHARLES DE GAULLE

Campaigns and battles are nothing but a long series of difficulties to be overcome. The lack of equipment, the lack of food, the lack of this or that are only excuses; the real leader displays his quality in his triumph over adversity, however great it may be.

GENERAL GEORGE MARSHALL

A piece of spaghetti or a military unit can only be led from the front end.

GENERAL GEORGE S. PATTON

Gentlemen, we are being killed on the beaches. Lets go inland and be killed.

GENERAL NORMAN COTA, Omaha Beach, 1944

I don't mind being called tough since I find in this racket it's the tough guys who lead the survivors.

GENERAL CURTIS E. LEMAY

"Bob . . . I want you to take Buna, or not come back alive."

GENERAL DOUGLAS MACARTHUR, to General Robert Eichelberger

There are two kinds of people, leaders and wingmen. A "manager" is a wingman you leave at home on the day of the big strike.

GENERAL RONALD R. FOGLEMAN

ℜ COMMAND AND LEADERSHIP ℘

No amount of study or learning will make a man a leader unless he has the natural qualities of one.

FIELD MARSHAL ARCHIBALD PERCIVAL WAVELL, First Earl Wavell

He who wishes to be obeyed must know how to command.

NICCOLO MACHIAVELLI

I can no longer obey; I have tasted command, and I cannot give it up.

NAPOLEON BONAPARTE

To command is to serve, nothing more, nothing less.

ANDRÉ MALRAUX

A chief is a man who assumes responsibility. He says, "I was beaten," he does not say "My men were beaten."

ANTOINE DE SAINT-EXUPÉRY

I must follow them. I am their leader.

ANDREW BONAR LAW

The most important quality in a leader is that of being acknowledged as such. All leaders whose fitness is questioned are clearly lacking in force.

ANDRÉ MAUROIS

Everyone imposes his own system as far as his army can reach.

JOSEPH STALIN

To a surprising extent the war-lords in shining armour, the apostles of martial virtues, tend not to die fighting when the time comes. History is full of ignominious getaways by the great and famous.

GEORGE ORWELL

It is not the business of generals to shoot one another.

ARTHUR WELLESLEY, Duke of Wellington

Name me an emperor who was ever struck by a cannonball.

CHARLES V, of France

All very successful commanders are prima donnas and must be so treated.

GENERAL GEORGE S. PATTON

Great leaders are almost always great simplifiers, who can cut through argument, debate and doubt, to offer a solution everybody can understand.

GENERAL COLIN POWELL

The true test of a leader is whether his followers will adhere to his cause from their own volition, enduring the most arduous hardships without being forced to do so, and remaining steadfast in the moments of greatest peril.

XENOPHON

Leadership in the democratic army means firmness, not harshness; understanding, not weakness; justice, not license; humaneness, not intolerance; generosity, not selfishness; pride, not egotism.

GENERAL OMAR BRADLEY

Always do everything you ask of those you command.

GENERAL GEORGE S. PATTON

Strength is leading when you just don't want to lead. You're leading by example. That's what we do. Particularly when it's really, really hard, and it hurts inside.

GENERAL STAN MCCHRYSTAL

Never neglect details. When everyone's mind is dulled or distracted the leader must be doubly vigilant.

GENERAL COLIN POWELL

To watch a highly skilled, experienced and resolute commander controlling a hard-fought battle is to see, not only a man triumphing over the highest mental and physical stresses, but an artist producing his effects in the most complicated and difficult of all the arts.

FIELD MARSHAL SIR WILLIAM J. SLIM

The nature of encounter operations required of the commanders limitless initiative and constant readiness to take the responsibility for military actions.

MARSHAL GEORGY ZHUKOV

Battles are won by slaughter and maneuver. The greater the general, the more he contributes in maneuver, the less he demands in slaughter.

WINSTON CHURCHILL

There is small risk a general will be regarded with contempt by those he leads, if, whatever he may have to preach, he shows himself best able to perform.

XENOPHON

Leadership is intangible, and therefore no weapon ever designed can replace it.

GENERAL OMAR BRADLEY

The more a general is accustomed to place heavy demands on his soldiers, the more he can depend on their response.

CARL VON CLAUSEWITZ

Few orders are best, but they should be followed up with care.

MAURICE DE SAXE

Remember, gentlemen, an order that can be misunderstood, will be misunderstood.

FIELD MARSHAL HELMUTH VON MOLTKE THE ELDER

Remember this: the truly great leader overcomes all difficulties, and campaigns and battles are nothing but a long series of difficulties to be overcome. The lack of equipment, the lack of food, the lack of this or that are only excuses: the real leader displays his quality in his triumphs over adversity, however great it may be.

GENERAL GEORGE MARSHALL

When things go wrong in your command, start searching for the reason in increasingly larger concentric circles around your own desk.

GENERAL BRUCE C. CLARKE

The principal task of the general is mental, involving large projects and major arrangements. But since the best dispositions become useless if they are not executed, it is essential that the general should be industrious in seeing whether his orders are executed or not.

FREDERICK THE GREAT

ஒ EXPERIENCE ஐ

It should be the duty of every soldier to reflect on the experiences of the past, in the endeavor to discover improvements, in his particular sphere of action, which are practicable in the immediate future.

B. H. LIDDELL HART

Judgment comes from experience, and experience comes from bad judgment.

SIMÓN BOLÍVAR

What is the good of experience if you do not reflect?

FREDERICK THE GREAT

The courage of a soldier is heightened by his knowledge of his profession.

VEGETIUS

But courage which goes against military expediency is stupidity, or, if it is insisted upon by a commander, irresponsibility.

GENERAL ERWIN ROMMEL

After Vietnam, we had a whole cottage industry develop basically in Washington D.C., that consisted of a bunch of military fairies that had never been shot at in anger, who felt fully qualified to comment on the leadership ability of all the leaders of the United States Army.

GENERAL NORMAN SCHWARTZKOPF, 1991 address to West Point cadets

❦ DISCIPLINE ❦

There is only one sort of discipline, perfect discipline.

GENERAL GEORGE S. PATTON

We find that the Romans owed the conquest of the world to no other cause than continual military training, exact observance of discipline in their camps, and unwearied cultivation of the other arts of war.

VEGETIUS

A well-disciplined regiment is as well behaved as a community of monks.

FREDERICK THE GREAT

Above all, discipline; eternally and inevitably, discipline. Discipline is the screw, the nail, the cement, the glue, the nut, the bolt, the rivet that holds everything tight. Discipline is the wire, the connecting rod, the chain that coordinates. Discipline is the oil that makes machines run fast, and the oil that makes parts slide smooth, as well as the oil that makes the metal bright. They know about discipline here. The principle of discipline is divinely simple; you lay it on thick and fast, all the time.

PRIVATE GERALD GERSH, Coldstream Guards

In no other profession are the penalties for employing untrained personnel so appalling and so irrevocable as in the military.

GENERAL DOUGLAS MACARTHUR

If you can't get them to salute when they should salute and wear the clothes you tell them to wear, how are you going to get them to die for their country?

GENERAL GEORGE S. PATTON

The core of the military profession is discipline and the essence of discipline is obedience. Reasonable orders are easy enough to obey; it is capricious, bureaucratic or plain idiotic demands that form the habit of discipline.

BARBARA TUCHMAN

For his own sake and for that of those around him, a man must be prepared for that awful, shrieking moment of truth when he realizes that he is all alone on a hill ten thousand miles from home, and that he may be killed in the next second.

T. R. FEHRENBACH

Bring them together by treating them humanely and keep them together with strict military discipline. This will assure their allegiance.

SUN TZU

Let officers and men be made to feel that they will most effectively secure their safety by remaining steadily at their posts, preserving order, and fighting with coolness and vigor.

GENERAL ROBERT E. LEE

Discipline is the soul of an army.

GEORGE WASHINGTON

The purpose of discipline is to make men fight in spite of themselves.

ARDANT DU PICQ, *Battle Studies*

Units fight well because of pride and training.

T. R. FEHRENBACH

Any army without discipline is no more than a mob, alternating between frightened sheep and beasts of prey.

FIELD MARSHAL SIR WILLIAM J. SLIM

Discipline, control from without, can only be relaxed safely when it is replaced by something higher and better, control from within.

CHARLES WILSON, First Baron Moran

Even if punishment and reward are applied circumspectly they certainly do not constitute a sufficient means of instituting and maintaining discipline. To achieve this, obedience must be given voluntarily rather than under compulsion.

XENOPHON

GENERALS AND ADMIRALS

I didn't fire him [General MacArthur] because he was a dumb son of a bitch, although he was, but that's not against the law for generals. If it was, half to three-quarters of them would be in jail.

HARRY S. TRUMAN

Ah! The Generals! They are numerous but not good for much!

ARISTOPHANES

An important difference between the military operation and a surgical operation is that the patient is not tied down. But it is a common fault of generalship to assume that he is.

B. H. LIDDELL HART

As for being a General, well, at the age of four with paper hats and wooden swords we're all Generals. Only some of us never grow out of it.

PETER USTINOV, *Romanoff and Juliet*

As matters stand now, a private who loses a rifle suffers far greater consequences than a general who loses a war.

LIEUTENANT COLONEL PAUL YINGLING

We make generals today on the basis of their ability to write a damned letter. Those kinds of men can't get us ready for war.

LIEUTENANT GENERAL LEWIS "CHESTY" PULLER

Congress can make a general but only communications can make him a commanding general.

GENERAL OMAR BRADLEY

The first advice I am going to give my successor is to watch the generals and to avoid feeling that just because they were military men their opinions on military matters were worth a damn.

JOHN F. KENNEDY

He smiles with the faraway, sea-remembering smile of all desk admirals.

PETER GRIER

An admiral has to be put to death now and then to encourage the others.

VOLTAIRE

It is dangerous to meddle with Admirals when they say they can't do things. They have always got the weather or fuel or something to argue about.

WINSTON CHURCHILL

If there's one thing I can't stand it's an intellectual admiral.

HENRY KISSINGER

I am convinced that the best service a retired general can perform is to turn in his tongue along with his suit and to mothball his opinion.

GENERAL OMAR BRADLEY

❧ COMMAND STAFFS ❧

A bulky staff implies a division of responsibility, slowness of action, and indecision, whereas a small staff implies activity and concentration of purpose.

GENERAL WILLIAM T. SHERMAN

The typical staff officer is a man past middle life, spare, wrinkled, intelligent, cold, noncommittal, with eyes like a codfish, polite in contact, but at the same time unresponsive, cool, calm and as damnably composed as a concrete post or plaster of Paris cast; a human petrifaction with a heart of feldspar and without charm or the friendly germ; minus bowels, passions or a sense of humor. Happily they never reproduce and all of them finally go to hell.

GENERAL GEORGE S. PATTON

Staffs analyze; commanders synthesize.

Anonymous

The greatest danger to the Staff College is a swollen head.

F. P. CROZIER

Never tell people how to do things. Tell them what to do and they will surprise you with their ingenuity.

GENERAL GEORGE S. PATTON

I must have assistants who will solve their own problems and tell me later what they have done.

GENERAL GEORGE MARSHALL

Any commander who fails to exceed his authority is not of much use to his subordinates.

ADMIRAL ARLEIGH A. BURKE

Organization doesn't really accomplish anything. Plans don't accomplish anything, either. Theories of management don't much matter. Endeavors succeed or fail because of the people involved. Only by attracting the best people will you accomplish great deeds.

GENERAL COLIN POWELL

Paperwork will ruin any military force.

LIEUTENANT GENERAL LEWIS "CHESTY" PULLER

The little affair of operational command is something anybody can do.

ADOLF HITLER

There is a weakness in a council running a war. That is true of any council. I don't care if it is composed of the best men in the world. . . . In war, you must have a decision. A bum decision is better than none. And the trouble is when you get three, you finally get none.

DWIGHT D. EISENHOWER

Nothing is more important in war than unity in command.

NAPOLEON BONAPARTE

❧ OFFICERS ❧

Officers can never act with confidence until they are masters of their profession.

HENRY KNOX

Since officers must necessarily lead them into the greatest dangers, the soldiers should fear their officers more than all the dangers to which they are exposed. Good will can never induce the common soldier to stand up to such dangers; he will only do so through fear.

FREDERICK THE GREAT

But ground battle is a series of platoon actions . . . Orders in combat—the orders that kill men or get them killed, are not given by generals, or even by majors. They are given by lieutenants and sergeants, and sometimes by PFC's [Privates First Class].

T. R. FEHRENBACH

The Gauls were not conquered by the Roman legions but by Caesar. It was not before the Carthaginian soldiers that Rome was made to tremble, but before Hannibal.

MAJOR GENERAL J. F. C. FULLER

In my experience . . . officers with high athletic qualifications are not usually successful in the higher ranks.

WINSTON CHURCHILL

The military officer is considered a gentleman, not because Congress will it . . . but specifically because nothing less than a gentleman is truly suited for his particular set of responsibilities.

S. L. A. MARSHALL

Every officer has his ceiling in rank, beyond which he should not be allowed to rise—particularly in war-time.

FIELD MARSHAL BERNARD MONTGOMERY

An army cannot be administered. It must be led.

FRANZ JOSEPH STRAUSS

The [military] officer is a being apart, a kind of artist breathing the grand air in the brilliant profession of arms, in a uniform that is always seductive. . . . To me the officer is a separate race.

MATA HARI

The Commander-in-Chief may be only a name to his army, but a battalion is at the mercy of its officers.

CHARLES WILSON, First Baron Moran

When a nation re-awakens, its finest sons are prepared to give their lives for its liberation. When empires are threatened with collapse, they are prepared to sacrifice their non-commissioned officers.

MENACHIM BEGIN

Wars may be fought with weapons, but they are won by men. It is the spirit of the men who follow and of the man who leads that gains the victory.

GENERAL GEORGE S. PATTON

Long ago I had learned that in conversation with an irate senior, a junior should confine himself to the three remarks, "yes, sir," "no, sir," and "sorry, sir." Repeated in the proper sequence, they will get him through the most difficult interview with the minimum discomfort.

FIELD MARSHAL SIR WILLIAM J. SLIM

Officers in France, the pick of them, seemed instinctively to realize, as time passed, that to get the best results out of their men they must appeal to the best that was in them.

CHARLES WILSON, First Baron Moran

Do what is right, not what you think the high headquarters wants or what you think will make you look good.

GENERAL NORMAN SCHWARTZKOPF

These clutch hitters [emergent combat leaders] are able to fill the void caused by a failure of appointed leadership because they do not mistake the appearance of that position for the reality.

S. L. A. MARSHALL

A man's actions and omissions spring first and foremost from his character and naturally, but to a lesser degree, from his origins, his upbringing, and his training. How a man appears to his superiors may differ markedly from his image in the eyes of his subordinates, who often see him in quite another light.

F.W. VON MELLENTHIN

First there is the All-Highest (the Kaiser), then the Cavalry Officer, and then the Cavalry Officer's horse. After that, there is nothing, and after nothing, is the Infantry Officer.

Imperial German Army saying

❧ ENLISTED MEN ❧

Battles are sometimes won by generals; wars are nearly always won by sergeants and privates.

F. E. ADCOCK

Soldiers win battles and generals get the credit.

NAPOLEON BONAPARTE

In combat, life is short, nasty and brutish. The issues of national policy which brought him into war are irrelevant to the combat soldier; he is concerned with his literal life chances.

CHARLES E. MOSKOS, JR.

They were learning the reality of war, these youngsters, getting face to face with the sickening realization that men get killed uselessly because their generals are stupid, so that desperate encounters where the last drop of courage has been given serve the country not at all and make a patriot look a fool.

BRUCE CATTON

Men and women who would shrink from doing anything dishonorable in the sphere of personal relationships are ready to lie and swindle and to steal and even murder when they are representing their country.

ALDOUS HUXLEY

It's one of the most serious things that can possibly happen to one in a battle—to get one's head cut off.

LEWIS CARROLL, *Through the Looking Glass*

They wish to hell they were someplace else, and they wish to hell they would get relief. They wish to hell the mud was dry and they wish to hell their coffee was hot. They want to go home. But they stay in their wet holes and fight, and then they climb out and crawl through minefields and fight some more.

BILL MAULDIN

They were called grunts, and many of them, however grudgingly, were proud of the name. They were the infantrymen, the foot soldiers of the war.

BERNARD EDELMAN

Men acquainted with the battlefield will not be found among the numbers that glibly talk of another war.

DWIGHT D. EISENHOWER

Look at an infantryman's eyes and you can tell how much war he has seen.

BILL MAULDIN

When a soldier sees a clean face there's one more whore in the world.

BERTOLT BRECHT

Another name for ground troops is targets, or hostages.

COLONEL PHILLIP S. MEILINGER

⬙ SAILORS ⬙

There were gentlemen and there were seamen in the navy of Charles the Second. But the seamen were not gentlemen; and the gentlemen were not seamen.

THOMAS BABINGTON MACAULAY

A soldier should be sworn to the patient endurance of hardships, like the ancient knights; and it is not the least of these necessary hardships to have to serve with sailors.

FIELD MARSHAL BERNARD MONTGOMERY

No man will be a sailor who has contrivance enough to get himself into a jail; for being in a ship is being in a jail, with the chance of being drowned. A man in jail has more room, better food, and commonly better company.

SAMUEL JOHNSON

◈ SOLDIERS ◈

The officers will take all proper opportunities to inculcate in their men's minds a reliance on the bayonet, men of their bodily strength and even a coward may be their match in firing. But a bayonet in the hands of the valiant is irresistible.

MAJOR GENERAL JOHN BURGOYNE

Tell them that this affair must hang in the balance no longer; sweep the field with the bayonet.

GENERAL THOMAS "STONEWALL" JACKSON, at Gaines Hill

"Why me?" That is the soldier's first question, asked each morning as the patrols go out and each evening as the night settles around the foxholes.

WILLIAM BROYLES, JR., *Brothers in Arms*

Every soldier generally thinks only as far as the radius of action of his branch of the service and only as quickly as he can move with his weapons.

LUFTWAFFE GENERAL KARL KOLLER

I never expect a soldier to think.

GEORGE BERNARD SHAW

When you put on a uniform, there are certain inhibitions that you accept.

DWIGHT D. EISENHOWER

Three-quarters of a soldier's life is spent in aimlessly waiting about.

EUGEN ROSENSTOCK-HUESSY

The chief attraction of military service has consisted and will consist in this compulsory and irreproachable idleness.

LEO TOLSTOY

Comradeship is based on affection and trust.

FIELD MARSHAL BERNARD MONTGOMERY

Four brave men who do not know each other will not dare to attack a lion. Four less brave, but knowing each other well, sure of their reliability and consequently of mutual aid, will attack resolutely.

ARDANT DU PICQ

The services in wartime are fit only for desperadoes, but in peace are fit only for fools.

BENJAMIN DISRAELI

We played remote bases, the kind of bases where guys went to bed with their rifles by their sides; not for safety, but for companionship.

BOB HOPE

No soldier can fight unless he is properly fed on beef and beer.

JOHN CHURCHILL, Duke of Marlborough, ca. 1710

My men can eat their belts, but my tanks have got to have gas.
GENERAL GEORGE S. PATTON

The road to glory cannot be followed with much baggage.
MAJOR GENERAL RICHARD S. EWELL

If you can't carry it, eat it, or shoot it, don't bring it.
Anonymous

You can always tell an old soldier by the insides of his holsters and cartridge boxes. The young ones carry pistols and cartridges: the old ones, grub.
GEORGE BERNARD SHAW

It is enough for the world to know that I am a soldier.
GENERAL WILLIAM T. SHERMAN

"What do you want to go back in the Army for?" she cried, getting her breath. "What did the Army ever do for you? Besides beat you up and treat you like scum, and throw you in jail like a criminal? What do you want to go back there for?"

"What do I want to go back there for?" Prewitt said wonderingly. "I'm a soldier."
JAMES JONES, *From Here to Eternity*

Old soldiers never die; they just fade away.
GENERAL DOUGLAS MACARTHUR, in a 1951 address to a joint session of Congress

◎ GAYS IN THE MILITARY ◎

Don't Ask, Don't Tell.

> CHARLES E. MOSKOS, Jr. advisor to Senator Sam Nunn, who first suggested the four-part phrase, "Don't ask, don't tell, don't seek, don't flaunt." It was adopted by the U.S. Military in 1994 as "Don't ask, don't tell, don't pursue," then shortened by the media to "Don't Ask, Don't Tell," or DADT.

"Don't Ask, Don't Tell" is not a joking matter. It is the only law that enforces shame.

> LIEUTENANT DAN CHOI, openly gay Iraq War veteran

Has this policy been ideal? No, it has not. But it has been effective.

> SENATOR JOHN MCCAIN

Why is it that, as a culture, we are more comfortable seeing two men holding guns than holding hands?

> ERNEST GAINES

You don't have to be straight to be in the military; you just have to be able to shoot straight.

> SENATOR BARRY GOLDWATER

My hope is that gays will be running the world, because then there would be no war. Just a greater emphasis on military apparel.

ROSEANNE BARR

It is my personal belief that allowing gays and lesbians to serve openly would be the right thing to do. No matter how I look at the issue . . . I cannot escape being troubled by the fact that we have in place a policy which forces young men and women to lie about who they are in order to defend their fellow citizens. . . . For me, it comes down to integrity—theirs as individuals and ours as an institution.

ADMIRAL MICHAEL MULLEN, at a Senate Committee hearing

The policy is an absurdity and borderline on being an obscenity. What it does is cause people to ask of themselves that they lie to themselves, that they pretend to be something that they are not. There is no empirical evidence that would indicate that it affects military cohesion. There is a lot of evidence to say that the biases of the past have been layered onto the United States Army.

CLIFFORD ALEXANDER, Former Secretary of the Army

Conversations I've held with service members make clear that, while the military remains a traditional culture, that tradition no longer requires banning open service by gays. There will undoubtedly be some teething pains, but I have no doubt our leadership can handle it.

GENERAL JOHN M. SHALIKASHVILI, Former Chairman of the Joint Chiefs of Staff

You're basically asserting that straight men and women in our military aren't professional enough to serve openly with gay troops while completing their military missions. You know as a former Army officer I can tell you I think that's an insult to me and to many of the soldiers. To answer your question, Mr. Jones, it was 24 countries that allow military personnel to serve openly without any detrimental impact on unit cohesion.

PATRICK MURPHY, Iraq War veteran and U.S. Congressman, challenging a witness during hearings in the U.S. House

Army values are taught to soldiers from their earliest days in the Army. Those values are: Loyalty, duty, mutual respect, selfless service, honor, integrity and personal courage. We teach our soldiers that these are the values we expect them to live up to. I believe that as an institution, our military needs to live up to the values we demand of the service members. Military leaders need to respect all service members. We need to recognize that loyalty and selfless service are exhibited equally, by service members of every color, gender and sexual orientation.

RETIRED LIEUTENANT GENERAL CLAUDIA KENNEDY

We have to correct this. It's just not right. I can remember being out there in command, and someone would come up to you and start to tell you—and you just want to say, no, I don't want to lose you, you're too good.

JOE SESTAK, Former Navy Vice Admiral and U.S. Congressman

Today, with implementation of the new law fully in place, we are a stronger joint force, a more tolerant joint force, a force of more character and more honor, more in keeping with our own values.

ADMIRAL MICHAEL MULLEN, Chairman of the Joint Chiefs of Staff

When I was in the military they gave me a medal for killing two men, and a discharge for loving one.

LEONARD MATLOVICH, Air Force sergeant who died of AIDS. Inscription is on his tombstone.

ᏣᎦ WOMEN AND THE MILITARY ᏍᎧ

My business is stanching blood and feeding fainting men; my post is the open field between the bullet and the hospital.

UNION NURSE CLARA BARTON, 1863, founder of the American Red Cross

I do have concerns about women in front line combat. I think that could be a very compromising situation where, where people naturally, you know, may do things that may not be in the interests of the mission because of other types of emotions that are involved.

SENATOR RICK SANTORUM

We have women in the military, but they don't put us in the front lines. They don't know if we can fight, if we can kill. I think we can. All the general has to do is walk over to the women and say, "You see the enemy over there? They say you look fat in those uniforms."

ELAYNE BOOSLER

As a woman I can't go to war, and I refuse to send anyone else.
JEANNETTE RANKIN, first woman in the U.S. House of Representatives. She lost her seat in Congress when she voted against entry in WWI.

I don't know how long before i shall have to go into the field of battle. For my part i don't care. I don't feel afraid to go. I don't believe there are any Rebel's bullets made for me yet.
PRIVATE LYONS WAKEMAN, 153rd Regiment, New York State Volunteers, 1862. Wakeman's real name was Sarah Rosetta Wakeman, who disguised her sex when she enlisted. She did not survive the war.

I asked a Burmese why women, after centuries of following their men, now walk ahead. He said there were many unexploded land mines since the war.

ROBERT MUELLER, Director of the FBI

There is no one more surprised than I—except, of course, my husband. You know what they say, "Behind every successful woman there is an astonished man."

LIEUTENANT GENERAL ANN E. DUNWOODY, upon her nomination for a fourth star

If I had learned to type, I never would have made Brigadier General.

BRIGADIER GENERAL ELIZABETH P. HOSINGTON

⊗ FIGHTER PILOTS ⊗

The will to fly was (and in many cases still is) the will to conquer, to overcome all obstacles in the effort to gain control over the natural conditions of environment.

M. J. BERNARD DAVY

Pilots are a rare kind of human. They leave the ordinary surface of the world, to purify their souls in the sky, and they come down to earth, only after receiving the communion of the infinite.

JOSE MARIA VELASCO IBARRA

Son, never ask a man if he is a fighter pilot. If he is, he'll let you know. If he isn't, don't embarrass him.

ROBERT DUVALL, as Lieutenant Colonel "Bull" Meecham in *The Great Santini*

I think it is love of that blue vault of sky that becomes your playground if, and only if, you are a fighter pilot. You don't understand it if you fly from A to B in straight and level, and merely climb and descend. You're moving through the basement of that bolt of blue.

BRIGADIER GENERAL ROBIN OLDS

I have flown in just about everything, with all kinds of pilots in all parts of the world—British, French, Pakistani, Iranian, Japanese, Chinese—and there wasn't a dime's worth of difference between any of them except for one, unchanging, certain fact: the best, most skillful pilot had the most experience.

ASTRONAUT CHUCK YEAGER

Among the many resources which contribute to effective airpower, only one, people, actually appreciates, rather than depreciates over time.

AIR VICE-MARSHAL TONY MASON

Very few of our pilots are wounded; they are killed.

BRIGADIER GENERAL BILLY MITCHELL

There won't be any "after the war" for a fighter pilot.

MAJOR RAOUL LUFBERRY, killed in action, 1918

⚘ SEA POWER ⚘

He who commands the sea has command of everything.

THEMISTOCLES

This much is certain, he that commands the sea is at great liberty and may take as much or as little of the war as he will, whereas those that be strongest by land are many times nevertheless in great straits.

SIR FRANCIS BACON, 1597

Without a decisive naval force we can do nothing definitive, and with it everything honorable and glorious.

GEORGE WASHINGTON

Wherever wood can swim, there I am sure to find this flag of England.

NAPOLEON BONAPARTE

We English have to regret that we cannot always decide the fate of Empires on the sea.

LORD HORATIO NELSON

If a nation be so situated that it is neither forced to defend itself by land nor induced to seek extension of its territory by way of the land, it has, by the very unity of its aim directed upon the sea, an advantage as compared with a people one of whose boundaries is continental.

ALFRED THAYER MAHAN

The object of naval warfare is the control of communications, and not, as in land warfare, the conquest of territory. The difference is fundamental.

SIR JULIAN CORBETT

Sea-power does not, as some forms of military power can, operate like a lightening flash. Its effect is more like radium, beneficial to those who are shielded, it destroys the tissues of those who are exposed to it.

B. H. LIDDELL HART

The Navy Department frequently seemed to retire from the realm of logic into a dim religious world in which Neptune was God, Mahan his prophet, and the United States Navy the only true Church.

HENRY L. STIMSON

The Third Fleet's sunken and damaged ships have been salvaged and are retiring at high speed toward the enemy.

ADMIRAL WILLIAM "BULL" HALSEY, JR., report after the Japanese claimed that the Third Fleet had been sunk, October 14, 1944

⊗ MEDALS ৵

A soldier will fight long and hard for a bit of colored ribbon.

NAPOLEON BONAPARTE

Civilians may think its a little juvenile to worry about ribbons, but a civilian has a house and a bankroll to show for what he's done for the past four years.

BILL MAULDIN

The world continues to offer glittering prizes to those who have stout hearts and sharp swords.

FREDERICK EDWIN SMITH, Earl of Birkenhead

After about 25 medals, you run out of shoulder to put them on.

U.S. AIR FORCE COLONEL GEORGE DAY

A chest full of medals is nothing more than a resume in 3-D and Technicolor.

OWEN EDWARDS

⊗ SOLDIERS AND WOMEN ৵

Men love war because it allows them to look serious, because it's the only thing that stops women from laughing at them.

JOHN FOWLES

Ask any soldier. To kill a man is to merit a woman.
JEAN GIRAUDOUX

The last thing a woman will consent to discover in a man whom she loves or on whom she simply depends, is want of courage.
JOSEPH CONRAD

None but the Brave deserves the Fair.
JOHN DRYDEN, "Alexander's Feast"

Join a Highland regiment, me boy. The kilt is an unrivaled garment for fornication and diarrhea.
LIEUTENANT COLONEL JOHN MASTERS

I can still hear the awful lamentation of the women and the drunken uproar of the men during the first days of war.
GENERAL PETRO GRIGORENKO

When the military man approaches, the world locks up its spoons and packs off its womankind.
GEORGE BERNARD SHAW

Treat your airplane like you would a woman. Climb inside her seven or eight times a day and take her to heaven and back.
CAPTAIN LORD FLASHHEART, in the BBC series *The Black Adder*

A good uniform must work its way with the women, sooner or later.

CHARLES DICKENS

I always like a man in uniform. . . . That one fits you perfect. Say, why don't you come up some time? I'm home every evening.

MAE WEST, *Diamond Lil*

The only war I ever approved of was the Trojan War; it was fought over a woman and the men knew what they were fighting for.

WILLIAM LYON PHELPS

❧ MOTHERS AND SONS ❧

I have already given two cousins to the war and I stand ready to sacrifice my wife's brother.

CHARLES FARRAR BROWNE (Artemus Ward)

The one thing I cannot forgive the Arabs for is that they forced our sons to kill their sons.

GOLDA MEIR

The time not to become a father is eighteen years before a war.

E. B. WHITE

Mother whose heart hung humble as a button
On the bright splendid shroud of your son,
Do not weep.
War is kind.

STEPHEN CRANE, "War Is Kind"

If there must be trouble let it be in my day, that my child may have peace.

THOMAS PAINE

In peace, sons bury their fathers; in war, fathers bury their sons.

HERODOTUS

War may make a fool of man, but it by no means degrades him; on the contrary, it tends to exalt him, and its net effects are much like those of motherhood on women.

H. L. MENCKEN

It's not what men fight for. They fight in the last resort to impress their mothers.

GABRIEL FIELDING

We fight for men and women whose poetry is not yet written.

COLONEL ROBERT GOULD SHAW

❧ THE ARMY, THE NAVY, THE AIR FORCE, THE MARINES ❧

The British Army should be a projectile fired by the British Navy.

SIR EDWARD GREY

In plain language, no soldier is competent to operate the Air, just as no airman is competent to operate the Army.

FIELD MARSHAL BERNARD MONTGOMERY, 1943

Never in history has the Navy landed an army at the planned time and place.

GENERAL GEORGE S. PATTON, November 1942

Why should we have a navy at all? There are no enemies for it to fight except apparently the Army Air Force.

GENERAL CARL SPAATZ

The greatest lesson of this war has been the extent to which air, land, and sea operations can and must be coordinated by joint planning and unified command. The attainment of better coordination and balance than now exists between services is an essential of national security.

GENERAL HENRY "HAP" ARNOLD

It [a joint committee] leads to weak and faltering decisions, or rather indecisions. Why, you may take the most gallant sailor, the most intrepid airman, or the most audacious soldier, put them at a table together, what do you get? The sum of their fears.

WINSTON CHURCHILL

A good inter-Service staff officer must first be a good officer of his own Service, and we should lose more than we gained by merging the identity of the three Staff Colleges.

MARSHAL OF THE RAF SIR JOHN C. SLESSOR

It takes close coordination with the Army to obtain maximum misuse of airpower.

GENERAL CARL SPAATZ, 1940

The function of the Army and Navy in any future war will be to support the dominant air arm.

GENERAL JIMMY DOOLITTLE

❀ THE ARMY ❀

It would undoubtedly be desirable if we could create an army of dependable and specially selected men of the best type. But in order to make an army we must not destroy the nation; it would be destruction to a nation if we were deprived of the best elements. As things are, the army must inevitably consist of the scum of the people and of all those for whom society has no use.

LORD ST. GERMAIN, French Minister of War, 1775

People are not *in* the Army, they *are* the Army.

GENERAL CREIGHTON W. ABRAMS

Join the army, see the world, meet interesting people, and kill them.

Unknown

Army life was rough. Would you believe it, they actually wanted me to pitch three times a week.

YANKEE PITCHER WHITEY FORD

The Army is always the same. The sun and the moon change, but the Army knows no seasons.

JOHN WAYNE, as Captain Nathan Brittles in *She Wore a Yellow Ribbon*

The army taught me some great lessons—to be prepared for catastrophe—to endure being bored—and to know that however fine a fellow I thought myself in my usual routine there were other situations in which I was inferior to men that I might have looked down upon had not experience taught me to look up.

OLIVER WENDELL HOLMES, JR.

For it's Tommy this, an' Tommy that, an'
"Chuck him out, the brute!"
But it's "Saviour of 'is country," when the
guns begin to shoot;

RUDYARD KIPLING, "Tommy"

And here is the lesson I learned in the army. If you want to do a thing badly, you have to work at it as though you want to do it well.

PETER USTINOV

If they make an Aunt Sally of our army they will get an Aunt Sally army.

CHARLES WILSON, First Baron Moran

☙ THE NAVY ❧

We have met the enemy and they are ours—two ships, two brigs, one schooner and one sloop.

ADMIRAL OLIVER PERRY, in a message to General William Henry Harrison on his victory in the battle for Lake Erie

We joined the Navy to see the world
And what did we see? We saw the sea.

IRVING BERLIN

Sighted sub, sank same.

NAVY PILOT DONALD MASON, after attacking German submarine, 1942

The Navy's a very gentlemanly business. You fire at the horizon to sink a ship and then you pull people out of the water and say, "Frightfully sorry, old chap."

WILLIAM GOLDING

Something must be left to chance; nothing is sure in a sea fight beyond all others.

LORD HORATIO NELSON

The Navy is a machine invented by geniuses, to be run by idiots.

HERMAN WOUK, *The Caine Mutiny*

Don't talk to me about naval tradition. It's nothing but rum, sodomy, and the lash.

WINSTON CHURCHILL

A ship is always referred to as she because it costs so much to keep one in paint and powder.

ADMIRAL CHESTER NIMITZ

You seldom hear of the fleets and then you hear a lot.

ADMIRAL JOHN MCCAIN

The marines have a way of making you afraid, not of dying but of not doing your job.

CAPTAIN BONNIE LITTLE, quoted in *Iwo Jima: Legacy of Valor*, by Bill Ross, 1985

Some people spend an entire lifetime wondering if they've made a difference. The Marines don't have that problem.

RONALD REAGAN

A ship without Marines is like a coat without buttons.

ADMIRAL DAVID G. FARRAGUT

❧ VETERANS ❧

The only war is the war you fought in. Every veteran knows that.

ALLAN KELLER

The object of war is to survive it.

JOHN IRVING

War is God's way of teaching Americans geography.

AMBROSE BIERCE

Wars are different from baseball games where, at the end of the game, the teams get dressed and leave the park.

HARRY S. TRUMAN

A man who is good enough to shed his blood for his country is good enough to be given a square deal afterwards. More than that no man is entitled to, and less than that no man shall have.

THEODORE ROOSEVELT

I was only good once—in a war. Some men should never come back from war.

JOHN DALL, as John Bagtry in *Another Part of the Forest*

One of the main effects of war, after all, is that people are discouraged from being characters.

KURT VONNEGUT

Anybody who thinks that war is pleasant . . . you know, the old veteran stuff. You know, the "War is great stuff." Well, it's great for the survivors—not great for the people who are killed in it.

BERNARD B. FALL

All the wrong people remember Vietnam. I think all the people who remember it should forget it, and all the people who forgot it should remember it.

MICHAEL HERR

I joined the army, and succeeded in killing about as many of the enemy as they of me.

CHARLES HENRY SMITH

❧ PLANNING ❧

When the leaders speak of peace
The common folk know
That war is coming.
When the leaders curse war
The mobilization order is already written out.

BERTOLT BRECHT

However absorbed a commander may be in the elaboration of his own thoughts, it is necessary sometimes to take the enemy into consideration.

WINSTON CHURCHILL

I have studied in detail the accounts of every damned one of his battles. I know exactly how he will react under any given circumstance. He hasn't the slightest idea what I'm going to do. Therefore, when the day comes, I'm going to whip the hell out of him.

GENERAL GEORGE S. PATTON

It is a disgrace that modern air forces are still shackled to a planning and execution cycle that lasts three days. We have tied our jets to a hot air balloon.

GENERAL MERRILL MCPEAK

In planning, never a useless move; in strategy, no step taken in vain.

CHEN HAO

If you're in a fair fight, you didn't plan it properly.

NICK LAPPOS

❦ DECISIONS ❧

In 40 hours I shall be in battle, with little information, and on the spur of the moment will have to make most momentous decisions. But I believe that one's spirit enlarges with responsibility and that, with God's help, I shall make them and make them right.

GENERAL GEORGE S. PATTON

After a battle is over people talk a lot about how decisions were methodically reached, but actually there's always a hell of a lot of groping around.

ADMIRAL FRANK FLETCHER

An educated guess is just as accurate and far faster than compiled errors.

GENERAL GEORGE S. PATTON

General McClellan is an admirable Engineer, but he seems to have a special talent for the stationary engine.

ABRAHAM LINCOLN

Quick decisions are unsafe decisions.

SOPHOCLES

The god of war hates those who hesitate.

EURIPIDES

Take time to deliberate, but when the time for action arrives, stop thinking and go on.

ANDREW JACKSON

A good plan executed now is better than a perfect plan executed next week.

GENERAL GEORGE S. PATTON

In action it is better to order than to ask.

SIR IAN HAMILTON

Don't let adverse facts stand in the way of a good decision.

GENERAL COLIN POWELL

Wars are not fought on drawing boards, nor are victories to be measured in pints. War is every whit as much a game of chance as a game of calculation: it is poker as well as chess, and even in chess there is no slide-rule certainty.

MAJOR GENERAL J. F. C. FULLER

❧ STRATEGY ☙

Sir, my strategy is one against ten, my tactics ten against one.

ARTHUR WELLESLEY, Duke of Wellington

I can always make it a rule to get there first with the most men.

NATHAN BEDFORD FORREST

If the enemy holds a hill with a battalion, give me two battalions and I'll take it, but at great cost in casualties. Give me a division and I'll take it without a fight.

GENERAL DWIGHT D. EISENHOWER

In the old strategy the leading idea was to concentrate superiority of force against a decisive point, in the new it is to distribute it in such a way that the enemy will be entangled in a tactical net. Again, whilst the former aimed at cutting an enemy off from his communications, the latter aims at cutting communications off from the enemy.

MAJOR GENERAL J. F. C. FULLER

Our strategy to go after this [Iraq's] army is very, very simple. First, we are going to cut it off, and then we are going to kill it.

GENERAL COLIN POWELL

The principals of war could, for brevity, be condensed into a single word: concentration.

B. H. LIDDELL HART

If they've been put there to fight, there are far too few. If they've been put there to be killed, there are far too many.

SENATOR ERNEST F. HOLLINGS

The first law of war is to preserve ourselves and destroy the enemy.

MAO TSE-TUNG

The U.S. has broken the second rule of war. That is, don't go fighting with your land army on the mainland of Asia. Rule One is don't march on Moscow. I developed these two rules myself.

FIELD MARSHAL BERNARD MONTGOMERY

Rules to live by in Iraq: Be polite, be professional, but have a plan to kill everybody you meet.

MAJOR GENERAL JAMES MATTHIS

While a stroke close to the rear of the opposing army is apt to have more effect on the minds of the enemy's troops, a stroke farther back tends to have more effect on the mind of the enemy commander, and it is in the minds of commanders that the issue of battles is really decided.

B. H. LIDDELL HART

The military object will not be to assault the outer casing of the enemy's armed forces, but the internal organs of command, intercommunication and supply. And as the whole of these and the fighting troops depend for their existence on the maintenance of political authority, and as political authority can be changed by the will of the people, the civil population becomes the main target.

MAJOR GENERAL J. F. C. FULLER

Strategy is the art of making use of time and space. Space we can recover; lost time, never.

NAPOLEON BONAPARTE

Strategy is finding a sonofabitch whom you rank and telling him to take a place, and relieving him if he doesn't.

GENERAL GEORGE S. PATTON

Leadership is a potent combination of strategy and character. But if you must be without one, be without the strategy.

GENERAL NORMAN SCHWARTZKOPF

As when snow is squeezed into a snowball, direct pressure has always the tendency to harden and consolidate the resistance of an opponent, and the more compact it becomes the more difficult it is to melt.

B. H. LIDDELL HART

When you surround an army, leave an outlet free. Do not press a desperate foe too hard.

SUN TZU

I know their game. First, the traders and the missionaries: then the ambassadors: then the cannon. It's better to go straight to the cannon.

TEWODROS II, Ethiopian Emperor

Our cards were speed and time, not hitting power, and these gave us strategical rather than tactical strength. Range is more to strategy than force.

T. E. LAWRENCE

Amateurs talk of strategy; professionals talk logistics.

Anonymous

I don't know what the hell this "logistics" is that [General George] Marshall is always talking about, but I want some of it.

ADMIRAL ERNEST JOSEPH KING, 1942

While the horizon of strategy is bounded by war, grand strategy looks beyond the war to the subsequent peace.

B. H. LIDDELL HART

◌ TACTICS ◌

Soldiers usually are close students of tactics, but rarely are they the students of strategy and practically never of war.

BERNARD BRODIE

A big butcher's bill is not necessarily evidence of good tactics.

FIELD MARSHAL ARCHIBALD PERCIVAL WAVELL, First Earl Wavell

In peace we concentrate so much on tactics that we are apt to forget that it is merely the handmaiden of strategy.

B. H. LIDDELL HART

Tactics are concerned with doing the job "right," higher levels of strategy are concerned with doing the "right" job.

DENNIS M. DREW AND DONALD M. SNOW

Therefore, when I have won a victory I do not repeat my tactics but respond to circumstances in an infinite variety of ways.

SUN TZU

Movement generates surprise, and surprise gives impetus to movement. For a movement which is accelerated or changes its direction inevitably carries with it a degree of surprise, even though it be unconcealed; while surprise smoothes the path of movement by hindering the enemy's counter-measures and counter-movements.

B. H. LIDDELL HART

Tactics are the cutting edge of strategy, the edge which chisels out the plan into the action; consequently, the sharper this edge, the clearer cut will be the result.

MAJOR GENERAL J. F. C. FULLER

There are not fifty ways of fighting, there is only one way: to be the conqueror.

ANDRÉ MALRAUX

History shows that army campaigns in undeveloped countries have often involved waging war against natural obstacles, rather than against a foe.

AIR MARSHAL E. J. KINGSTON-MCCLOUGHRY

℘ MOBILITY AND FLEXIBILITY ℘

Aircraft carriers are very maneuverable; they can move to the left, to the right, and down.

GENERAL CARL SPAATZ, 1946

Nothing is more difficult than the art of maneuver. What is difficult about maneuver is to make the devious route the most direct and turn misfortune to advantage.

SUN TZU

Build no more fortresses, build railways.

FIELD MARSHAL HELMUTH VON MOLTKE THE ELDER

Movement is the safety-valve of fear.

B. H. LIDDELL HART

It is because blockade, like stockade, is a static conception adhered to in an age of ever-increasing mobility that, as a means of waging war, its values are on the wane.

MAJOR GENERAL J. F. C. FULLER

Air forces can be switched from one objective to another. They are not committed to any one course of action as an army is, by its bulk, complexity, and relatively low mobility. While their action should be concentrated, it can be quickly concentrated afresh against other objectives, not only in a different place, but of a different kind.

B. H. LIDDELL HART

Flexibility: A large general-purpose tent under which chaos, confusion and incompetency are kept well hidden.

GENERAL CREIGHTON W. ABRAMS

ৰ্জ MILITARY INTELLIGENCE ৯৩

Military intelligence is a contradiction in terms.

GROUCHO MARX

When the fate of a nation and the lives of its soldiers are at stake, gentlemen do not read each other's mail—if they can get their hands on it.

ALLEN DULLES, Director of Central Intelligence

Grand strategy depends upon policy, and policy upon political knowledge of war. If this knowledge is nil, policy will be nil, and grand strategy will follow suit. In other words, generalship becomes impossible.

MAJOR GENERAL J. F. C. FULLER

Nothing is more worthy of the attention of a good general than the endeavor to penetrate the designs of the enemy.

NICCOLO MACHIAVELLI

They have a saying in Chicago: "Once is happenstance. Twice is coincidence. The third time is enemy action."

IAN FLEMING, *Goldfinger*

Force and Fraud are in war the two cardinal virtues.

THOMAS HOBBES

One should know one's enemies, their alliances, their resources and nature of their country, in order to plan a campaign.

FREDERICK THE GREAT

How can any man say what he should do himself if he is ignorant what his adversary is about?

BARON ANTOINE-HENRI JOMINI

To lack intelligence is to be in the ring blindfolded.

GENERAL D. M. SHOUP

✺ ADAPTING AND INNOVATING ✺

Victory smiles upon those who anticipate the changes in the
character of war, not upon those who wait to adapt themselves after the changes occur.

ITALIAN GENERAL GIULIO DOUHET, *The Command of the Air*

Changes in military systems come about only through the
pressure of public opinion or disaster in war.

BRIGADIER GENERAL BILLY MITCHELL

The last war is not modern, it is out of date. At the same time,
there are factors that do not change, or only change very slowly.

Geography does not change—though its effects on military operations may be modified by technical changes. Human nature does not change, and national characteristics and temperaments change but slowly. Economic factors, generally speaking, change slowly.

MARSHAL OF THE RAF SIR ARTHUR TEDDER

The traditions among all the armed services are much older than any government, more conservative than any department of government, and more sure to build on a foundation that they are certain of, rather than take any chance of making a mistake.

BRIGADIER GENERAL BILLY MITCHELL

Dead battles, like dead generals, hold the military mind in their dead grip and Germans, no less than other peoples, prepare for the last war.

BARBARA TUCHMAN, *The Guns of August*

The only thing harder than getting a new idea into the military mind is to get an old one out.

B. H. LIDDELL HART

Those who study warfare only in the light of history think of the next war in terms of the last. But those who neglect history deprive themselves of a yardstick by which theory can be measured.

CYRIL FALLS

The value of history in the art of war is not only to elucidate the resemblance of the past and present, but also their essential differences.

SIR JULIAN CORBETT

If there is one attitude more dangerous than to assume that a future war will be just like the last one, it is to imagine that it will be so utterly different we can afford to ignore all the lessons of the last one.

GROUP CAPTAIN JOHN C. SLESSOR

In the development of airpower one has to look ahead and not backwards and figure out what is going to happen, not too much what has happened.

BRIGADIER GENERAL BILLY MITCHELL

Nothing so comforts the military mind as the maxim of a great, but dead, general.

BARBARA TUCHMAN

Out-of-date theories have consistently proved the ruin of armies.

MAJOR GENERAL J. F. C. FULLER

Nothing remains static in war or in military weapons, and it is consequently often dangerous to rely on courses suggested by apparent similarities in the past.

ADMIRAL ERNEST JOSEPH KING

I am tempted to declare that whatever doctrine the Armed Forces are working on, they have got it wrong. I am also tempted to declare that it does not matter that they have got it wrong. What does matter is their capacity to get it right quickly, when the moment arrives.

SIR MICHAEL HOWARD

An army is an institution not merely conservative but retrogressive by nature. It has such natural resistance to progress that it is always insured against the danger of being pushed ahead too fast.

B. H. LIDDELL HART

It is a sad comment, but the fact is indisputable that, after every war, preparation for the next war falls into the hands of those who have come least into contact with reality, the Generals and Staff Officers who directed the war from a distance, and not into the hands of those who lived in it cheek by jowl.

MAJOR GENERAL J. F. C. FULLER

It is ever a paradox in military affairs that the only way to obtain license for intellectual ideas is to prove oneself an expert in conventional practices.

B. H. LIDDELL HART

The peril of the hour moved the British to tremendous exertions, just as always in a moment of extreme danger things can be done which had previously been thought impossible. Mortal danger is an effective antidote for fixed ideas.

FIELD MARSHAL ERWIN ROMMEL

Since all progress is necessarily a matter of omitting old ways and adopting new, the first essential of leadership is a sublime indifference to precedent.

ROBERT QUILLEN

A good soldier, whether he leads a platoon or an army, is expected to look backward as well as forward, but he must think only forward.

GENERAL DOUGLAS MACARTHUR

❧ RETREAT ❧

The proper response to difficulty is not to retreat. It is to prevail.

GEORGE W. BUSH

Retreat hell! We're just attacking in another direction.

ATTRIBUTED TO MAJOR GENERAL OLIVER P. SMITH, Korea, December 1950.

Retreat hell! We just got here.

ATTRIBUTED TO CAPTAIN LLOYD WILLIAMS, USMC, Belleau Woods, June 5, 1918

There are few generals that have run oftener or more lustily than I have done. But I have taken care not to run too far, and commonly have run as fast forward as backward, to convince the Enemy that we were like a Crab, that could run either way.

NATHANAEL GREENE, to Henry Knox, 1781

They've got us surrounded again, the poor bastards.

GENERAL CREIGHTON W. ABRAMS

We have the enemy surrounded. We are dug in and have overwhelming numbers, but enemy airpower is mauling us badly. We will have to withdraw.

Japanese infantry commander, situation report to headquarters, Burma, World War II

◉ ORIGINALITY IN WAR ◎

Originality is the most vital of all military virtues, as two thousand years of wars attest. In peace it is at a discount, for it causes the disturbance of comfortable ways without producing dividends, as in civil life. But in war originality bears a higher premium than it can ever do in a civil profession. For its application can overthrow a nation and change the course of history in the proverbial twinkling of an eye.

B. H. LIDDELL HART

Originality, not conventionality, is one of the main pillars of generalship.

MAJOR GENERAL J. F. C. FULLER

You will usually find that the enemy has three courses open to him, and of these he will adopt the fourth.

FIELD MARSHAL HELMUTH VON MOLTKE THE ELDER

Successful generals make plans to fit the circumstances, but do not try to create circumstances to fit plans.

GENERAL GEORGE S. PATTON

Innovation is the bridge between doctrine and war.

MAJOR WILLIAM A. ANDREWS

If we wish to think clearly we must cease imitating; if we wish to cease imitating, we must make use of our imagination.

MAJOR GENERAL J. F. C. FULLER

❧ ATTRITION ❧

To adopt the method of attrition is not only a confession of stupidity, but a waste of strength, endangering both the chances during the combat and the profit of victory.

B. H. LIDDELL HART

Attrition is not strategy. It is in fact, irrefutable proof of the absence of any strategy.

LIEUTENANT GENERAL DAVID R. PALMER

The greatest secret of war and the masterpiece of a skillful general is to starve the enemy.

FREDERICK THE GREAT

Thus progressive butchery, politely called "attrition," becomes the essence of war. To kill, if possible, more of the enemy troops than your own side loses, is the sum total of this military creed, which attained its tragi-comic climax on the Western front in the Great War.

B. H. LIDDELL HART

A belligerent who limits himself to defense alone can only expect to win by attrition.

MARTIN VAN CREVELD

You will kill ten of our men and we will kill one of yours, and in the end it will be you who tire of it.

HO CHI MINH

MISTAKES IN WARFARE

War is the unfolding of miscalculations.

BARBARA TUCHMAN

War is mainly a catalogue of blunders.

WINSTON CHURCHILL

War is a series of catastrophes which result in victory.

GEORGES CLEMENCEAU

When a general makes no mistakes in war, it is because he has not been at it long.

MARSHAL HENRI DE LA TOUR D'AUVERGNE, Viconte de Turenne

Never interrupt your enemy when he is making a mistake.

NAPOLEON BONAPARTE

Any fool can profit from his own mistakes. The wise man profits from those of others.

OTTO VON BISMARCK

Our warfighting concept has to take account of the fact that almost nothing ever works right. As with the game of golf, our only real hope is to make smaller mistakes.

GENERAL MERRILL MCPEAK

Nothing is easy in war. Mistakes are always paid for in casualties and troops are quick to sense any blunders made by their comrades.

DWIGHT D. EISENHOWER, *Crusade in Europe*

To inquire if and where we made mistakes is not to apologize. War is replete with mistakes because it is full of improvisations. In war we are always doing something for the first time.

It would be a miracle if what we improvised under the stress of war should be perfect.

VICE ADMIRAL HYMAN RICKOVER

War is composed of nothing but accidents, and though holding to general principals, a general should never lose sight of everything to enable him to profit from those accidents; that is the mark of genius.

NAPOLEON BONAPARTE

ᐊᗕ AVOIDING THE FIGHT ᗒᐅ

The supreme excellence is not to win a hundred victories in a hundred battles. The supreme excellence is to subdue the armies of your enemies without even having to fight them.

SUN TZU

I do not favor battles, particularly at the beginning of a war. I am sure a good general can make war *all his life* and not be compelled to fight one.

MARSHAL MAURICE DE SAXE

True economy of force is using the indirect approach to effect a psychological defeat without engaging in actual combat.

B. H. LIDDELL HART

There are some roads not to follow; some troops not to strike; some cities not to assault; and some ground which should not be contested.

SUN TZU

Never wrestle with pigs—you get dirty and they enjoy it.

GENERAL CREIGHTON W. ABRAMS

❧ WAR ☙

War is, at first, the hope that one will be better off; next, the expectation that the other fellow will be worse off; then, the satisfaction that he isn't any better off; and, finally, the surprise at everyone's being worse off.

KARL KRAUS

War means ugly mob-madness, crucifying the truthtellers, choking the artists, sidetracking reforms, revolutions, and the working of social forces.

JOHN REED

It simply is not true that war never settles anything.

JUDGE FELIX FRANKFURTER

It is well that war is so terrible—we would grow too fond of it.

GENERAL ROBERT E. LEE

We are all familiar with the argument: Make war dreadful enough, and there will be no war. And we none of us believe it.

JOHN GALSWORTHY

War is not an adventure. It is a disease. It is like typhus.

ANTOINE DE SAINT-EXUPÉRY

They were going to look at war, the red animal—war, the blood-swollen god.

STEPHEN CRANE, *The Red Badge of Courage*

I have seen war. I have seen war on land and sea. I have seen blood running from the wounded. I have seen men coughing out their gassed lungs. I have seen the dead in the mud. I have seen cities destroyed. . . . I have seen children starving. I have seen the agony of mothers and wives. I hate war.

FRANKLIN D. ROOSEVELT

The more horrible a depersonalized scientific mass war becomes, the more necessary it is to find universal ideal motives to justify it.

JOHN DEWEY

The human race's prospects of survival were considerably better when we were defenseless against tigers than they are today when we have become defenseless against ourselves.

ARNOLD TOYNBEE

When a nation shows a civilized horror of war, it receives directly the punishment of its mistake. God changes its sex, despoils it of its common mark of virility, changes it into a feminine nation and sends conquerors to ravish it of its honour.

DONOSO CORTÉS

War alone brings up to its highest tension all human energy, and puts the stamp of nobility upon the peoples who have the courage to meet it. All other trials are substitutes, which never really put men into the position where they have to make the great decision—the alternatives of life or death.

BENITO MUSSOLINI

War is like love, it always finds a way.

BERTOLT BRECHT

Usually, when a lot of men get together, it's called war.

MEL BROOKS

For want of a nail the shoe was lost.
For want of a shoe the horse was lost.
For want of a horse the rider was lost.
For want of a rider the message was lost.
For want of a message the battle was lost.

BENJAMIN FRANKLIN

A battle sometimes decides everything, and sometimes the most trifling thing decides the fate of a battle.

NAPOLEON BONAPARTE

In war trivial causes produce momentous events.
JULIUS CAESAR

War is an obscene blot on the face of the human race.
SECRETARY OF STATE DEAN RUSK

WAR IS DELIGHTFUL

War is delightful to those who have had no experience of it.
ERASMUS

Let me have war, say I; it exceeds peace as far as day does night; it's spritely, waking, audible, and full of vent. Peace is a very apoplexy, lethargy: mulled, deaf, sleepy, insensible; a getter of more bastard children than war's a destroyer of men.
WILLIAM SHAKESPEARE, *Coriolanus*

Man lives by habits indeed, but what he lives for is thrill and excitements. . . . From time immemorial war has been . . . the supremely thrilling excitement.
WILLIAM JAMES

The grass grows green on the battlefield, but never on the scaffold.
WINSTON CHURCHILL

I love war and responsibility and excitement. Peace is going to be hell on me.

GENERAL GEORGE S. PATTON

War, when you are at it, is horrible and dull. It is only when time has passed that you see that its message was divine.

OLIVER WENDELL HOLMES, JR.

'Tis better to have fought and lost,
Than never to have fought at all.

ARTHUR HUGH CLOUGH

People who are vigorous and brutal often find war enjoyable, provided that it is a victorious war and that there is not too much interference with rape and plunder. This is a great help in persuading people that wars are righteous.

BERTRAND RUSSELL

I know I am among civilized men because they are fighting so savagely.

VOLTAIRE

I heard the bullets whistle, and believe me, there is something charming in the sound.

GEORGE WASHINGTON

Nothing is more exhilarating than to be shot at without result.

WINSTON CHURCHILL

I love the smell of napalm in the morning. . . . It smells like victory.

ROBERT DUVALL, as Lieutenant Colonel Bill Kilgore in *Apocalypse Now*

I love combat. I hate war. I don't understand it, but that's the way it is.

GENERAL CHARLES HORNER

It is not merely cruelty that leads men to love war, it is excitement.

HENRY WARD BEECHER

The statistics of suicide show that, for non-combatants at least, life is more interesting in war than in peace.

WILLIAM RALPH INGE

The only people who ever loved war for long were profiteers, generals, staff officers and whores.

ERNEST HEMINGWAY

To choose one's victim, to prepare one's plan minutely, to slake an implacable vengeance, and then go to bed. . . . There is nothing sweeter in the world.

JOSEPH STALIN

The greatest pleasure is to vanquish your enemies and chase them before you, to rob them of their wealth and see those dear to them bathed in tears, to ride their horses and clasp to your bosom their wives and daughters.

GENGHIS KHAN

◌ WAR IS HELL ◌

There is many a boy here today who looks on war as all glory, but boys, it is all hell.

GENERAL WILLIAM T. SHERMAN

War is the greatest plague that can afflict humanity; it destroys religion, it destroys states, it destroys families. Any scourge is preferable to it.

MARTIN LUTHER

How vile and despicable war seems to me! I would rather be hacked in pieces than take part in such an abominable business.

ALBERT EINSTEIN

We used to wonder where war lived, what it was that made it so vile. And now we realize that we know where it lives, that it is inside ourselves.

ALBERT CAMUS

Have you ever thought that war is a madhouse and that everyone in the war is a patient?

ORIANA FALLACI

I detest war. It spoils armies.

GRAND DUKE CONSTANTINE OF RUSSIA

ᙊ OFFENSIVE ACTION ᙎ

War, once declared, must be waged offensively, aggressively. The enemy must not be fended off, but smitten down.

ALFRED THAYER MAHAN

In war as in love, we must achieve contact ere we triumph.

NAPOLEON BONAPARTE

A conqueror, like a cannon-ball, must go on. If he rebounds, his career is over.

ARTHUR WELLESLEY, Duke of Wellington

No one thinking soundly, logically, would construct a strategic framework with offense only. Not the New York Giants. Not America.

GENERAL COLIN POWELL

So it happened that the spirit of the unlimited offensive smote us like the Black Death: we began once again to think in terms of numbers in place of skill and of quantity in place of quality.

MAJOR GENERAL J. F. C. FULLER

Not only strike while the iron is hot, but make it hot by striking.

OLIVER CROMWELL

Thrice armed is he that hath his quarrel just;
And four times he who gets his fist in fust.

CHARLES FARRAR BROWNE (Artemus Ward)

When you see a rattlesnake poised to strike, you do not wait until he has struck before you crush him.

FRANKLIN D. ROOSEVELT

I will soon commence on Loudon County, and let them know there is a God in Israel.

GENERAL PHILIP H. SHERIDAN

I have the finest army the sun ever shone on. I can march this army to New Orleans. My plans are perfect, and when I start to carry them out, may God have mercy on General Lee, for I will have none.

MAJOR GENERAL JOSEPH HOOKER, on the eve of Chancellorsville

We must therefore resign ourselves to the offensives the enemy inflicts upon us, while striving to put all our resources to work in inflicting even heavier ones upon him.

ITALIAN GENERAL GIULIO DOUHET

When Grant once gets possession of a place, he holds on to it as if he had inherited it.

ABRAHAM LINCOLN

My right is driven in, my center is giving way, the situation is excellent, I attack.

GENERAL MARSHAL FERDINAND FOCH, during the Battle of the Marne

The argument that "defence always catches up with attack" is much favoured by those who are opposed to progressive developments, even in the means of defence. History justifies it to a certain extent. But the assertion overlooks the historical fact that defence has often failed to catch up in time to save armies and navies, and the countries they are intended to protect, from defeat in the interval.

B. H. LIDDELL HART

The chief assets of the attacker are: firstly, the feeling of moral superiority which an offensive attitude gives, similar to that of the boxer who carries the fight to his opponent; and, secondly, the power to choose at what place, by what method, and at what time the main action will be fought.

FIELD MARSHAL ARCHIBALD PERCIVAL WAVELL, First Earl Wavell

We are having one of the loveliest battles you ever saw. It is a typical cavalry action in which the soldier went out and charged in all directions at the same time, with a pistol in one hand and saber in the other.

GENERAL GEORGE S. PATTON

❧ MODERATION ❧

Extremism in the defense of liberty is no vice. Moderation in the pursuit of justice is no virtue.

SENATOR BARRY GOLDWATER

Do not hit at all if it can be avoided, but never hit softly.

THEODORE ROOSEVELT

He knew that the essence of war is violence, and that moderation in war is imbecility.

THOMAS BABINGTON MACAULAY

Every attempt to make war easy and safe will result in humiliation and disaster.

GENERAL WILLIAM T. SHERMAN

I sincerely wish war was a pleasanter and easier business than it is, but it does not admit of holidays.

ABRAHAM LINCOLN, on the suggestion that he take a holiday

Well, we did not build those bombers to carry crushed rose petals.

GENERAL THOMAS S. POWER

If the people raise a howl against my barbarity and cruelty, I will answer that war is war, and not popularity-seeking.

If they want peace, they and their relatives must stop the war.

GENERAL WILLIAM T. SHERMAN

∝ SPEED IN WAR ∾

Just as lightning has already struck when the flash is seen, so when the enemy discovers the head of the army, the whole should be there, and leave him no time to counteract its dispositions.

JACQUES DE GUIBERT

Of all qualities in war it is speed which is dominant, speed both of mind and movement, without which hitting-power is valueless and with which it is multiplied.

B. H. LIDDELL HART

He who can move twice as fast as his opponent doubles his operative time and thereby halves that of his opponent.

MAJOR GENERAL J. F. C. FULLER

In order not to be left behind, we must work fast, clay feet are irreconcilable with the lightness of wings.

ITALIAN GENERAL GIULIO DOUHET

Again, speed in action must be cultivated; the power to think quickly in an emergency is one of the greatest assets both of the boxer and the commander; and the power to move quickly often gives to a body of troops, as to a boxer, the advantage of surprise.

FIELD MARSHAL ARCHIBALD PERCIVAL WAVELL, First Earl Wavell

Go sir, gallop, and don't forget that the world was made in six days. You can ask me for anything you like, except time.

NAPOLEON BONAPARTE

Time is the most precious element in war, and the saving of it by all possible means is the surest test of a good commander.

FIELD MARSHAL ARCHIBALD PERCIVAL WAVELL, First Earl Wavell

The history of failure in war can be summed up in two words: too late. Too late in comprehending the deadly purpose of a potential enemy; too late in realizing the mortal danger; too late in preparedness; too late in uniting all possible forces for resistance; too late in standing with one's friends.

GENERAL DOUGLAS MACARTHUR

When you engage in actual fighting, if victory is long in coming, the men's weapons will grow dull and their ardor dampened. Again, if the campaign is protracted the resources of the state will not be equal to the strain. Thus, though we have heard of stupid haste in war, cleverness has never been associated with long delays. There is no instance of a country having benefited from prolonged warfare.

SUN TZU

Time is the condition to be won to defeat the enemy. Time ranks first among the three factors necessary for victory, coming before terrain and support of the people. Only with time can we defeat the enemy.

HO CHI MINH

❧ WARS ENDING ❧

When war is over the first emotion is relief, the second, disappointment.

IAIN GLEN, as Sir Richard Carlisle in *Downton Abbey*

War involves in its progress such a train of unforeseen and unsupposed circumstances that no human wisdom can calculate the end. It has but one thing certain, and that is to increase taxes.

THOMAS PAINE

It's silly talking about how many years we will have to spend in the jungles of Vietnam when we could pave the whole country and put parking stripes on it and still be home by Christmas.

RONALD REAGAN

I could have ended the war in a month. I could have made North Vietnam look like a mud puddle.

SENATOR BARRY GOLDWATER

My solution to the problem [Vietnam] would be to tell them frankly that they've got to draw in their horns and stop their aggression, or we're going to bomb them back into the Stone Age.

GENERAL CURTIS E. LEMAY

The quickest way of ending a war is to lose it.

GEORGE ORWELL

Over? Did you say "over"? Nothing is over until we decide it is! Was it over when the Germans bombed Pearl Harbor? Hell no!

JOHN BELUSHI, as John "Blutto" Blutarsky in *Animal House*

∽ ARMAMENTS ∾

History shows us that no entirely new weapon has radically affected the course of any war; that the decisive weapon in a war has always been known, if but in a crude and undeveloped form, in the previous war.

B. H. LIDDELL HART

The more mechanical become the weapons with which we fight, the less mechanical must be the spirit which controls them.

MAJOR GENERAL J. F. C. FULLER

For Clausewitz, in his masterly analysis of the mental and physical spheres of war, neglected the material, man's tools. If he thereby ensured to his work an enduring permanence, he also, if unwittingly, ensured permanent injury to subsequent generations who allowed themselves to forget that the spirit cannot win battles when the body has been killed through failure to provide it with up-to-date weapons.

B. H. LIDDELL HART

(Armaments) constitute one of the most dangerous contributing causes of international suspicion and discord, and are calculated eventually to lead to war.

CALVIN COOLIDGE

The moral is obvious; it is that great armaments lead inevitably to war.

SIR EDWARD GREY

It is not armaments that cause war, but war that causes armaments.

SALVADOR DE MADARIAGA

Do what you can, with what you have, where you are.

THEODORE ROOSEVELT

You go to war with the army you have—not the army you might want or wish to have at a later time.

DONALD RUMSFELD

There are no manifestos like cannon and musketry.

ARTHUR WELLESLEY, Duke of Wellington

Guns before butter. Guns will make us powerful; butter will only make us fat.

HERMANN GOERING

Our swords shall play the orators for us.

CHRISTOPHER MARLOWE

All they that take the sword shall perish with the sword.

MATTHEW 26:52

Never fly the "A" model of anything.

EDWARD THOMPSON

The only time an aircraft has too much fuel on board is when it is on fire.

SIR CHARLES KINGSFORD SMITH

Why can't they buy just one airplane and take turns flying it?

CALVIN COOLIDGE

The Russians can give you arms, but only the United States can give you a selection.

ANWAR SADAT

⟋ CAPITALISM ⟍

The economy of a country resembles a masterpiece of precision mechanics: once it falls into disorder, interference, friction and breakages continue incessantly.

ADMIRAL HENNING VON HOLTZENDORFF, Chief of German Admiralty Staff, 1916

When the rich wage war, it is the poor who die.

JEAN-PAUL SATRE

Boys are the cash of war. Whoever said we're not free-spenders doesn't know our likes.

JOHN CIARDI

War is the trade of kings.

JOHN DRYDEN

Sooner or later every war of trade becomes a war of blood.

EUGENE V. DEBS

I want the whole of Europe to have one currency; it will make trading much easier.

NAPOLEON BONAPARTE, in a letter to Louis Bonaparte, May 6, 1807

Human beings do not fight for economic systems: who would be willing to die for capitalism? Certainly not the capitalists.

SIDNEY HOOK

When it comes time to hang the capitalists they will compete with each other to sell us the rope at a lower price.

VLADIMIR ILYICH LENIN

War is capitalism with the gloves off.

TOM STOPPARD

In time of war the loudest patriots are the greatest profiteers.

AUGUST BEBEL, German politician

Frankly, I'd like to see the government get out of war altogether and leave the whole field to private industry.

JOSEPH HELLER, *Catch-22*

To wage war, you need first of all money; second, you need money, and third, you also need money.

PRINCE RAIMONDO MONTECUCCOLI

We don't want to fight,
but, by jingo if we do.
We've got the ships, we've got the men,
we've got the money too.
"Macdermott's War Song," a British music-hall song
from which the word "jingoism" came

The sinews of war are five—men, money, material, maintenance (food) and morale.

BERNARD M. BARUCH

The sinews of war are infinite money.
CICERO

Money is the sinews of love, as of war.
GEORGE FARQUHAR, playwright

Wars are not paid for in wartime, the bill comes later.
BENJAMIN FRANKLIN

We must guard against the acquisition of unwarranted influence . . . by the military industrial complex. The potential for the disastrous rise of misplaced power exists and will persist.
DWIGHT D. EISENHOWER

You have to remember, we don't have the military industrial complex that we once had, when President Eisenhower spoke about it.
RONALD REAGAN

We are not self-employed.
GENERAL DAVID PETRAEUS, in response to a question of how he would advise the next President on Iraq

❧ PREDICTIONS ❧

Engines of war have long since reached their limits, and I see no further hope of any improvement in the art.
FRONTINUS, A.D. 90

It is not necessarily impossible for human beings to fly, but it so happens that God did not give them the knowledge of how to do it. It follows, therefore, that anyone who claims that he can fly must have sought the aid of the devil. To attempt to fly is therefore sinful.

ROGER BACON, ca. 1280

For I dipt into the future, far as human eye could see,
Saw the vision of the world, and all the wonder that
would be;
Saw the heavens fill with commerce, argosies of magic
sails,
Pilots of the purple twilight, dropping down with
costly bales;
Heard the heavens fill with shouting, and there rain'd
a ghastly dew,
From the nations' airy navies grappling in the central
blue.

ALFRED, LORD TENNYSON, "Locksley Hall," 1842

I tell you Wellington is a bad general, the English are bad soldiers; we will settle the matter by lunch time.

NAPOLEON BONAPARTE, the morning of the Battle of Waterloo

It is apparently not possible for another real war among the nations of Europe to take place.

DAVID STARR JORDAN, 1914

Has there ever been danger of war between Germany and ourselves, members of the same Teutonic race? Never has it even been imagined.

ANDREW CARNEGIE

Cavalry will never be scrapped to make room for the tanks; in the course of time cavalry may be reduced as the supply of horses in this country diminishes. This depends greatly on the life of fox-hunting.

British Army officer, writing in the *Journal of the Royal United Service Institute*, February 1921

Some enthusiasts today talk about the probability of the horse become extinct and prophesy that the aeroplane, the tank, and the motor car will supercede the horse in future wars. I am sure that as time goes on you will find just as much use for the horse, the well bred horse, as you have done in the past.

FIELD MARSHAL LORD DOUGLAS HAIG, 1925

I think it is well for the man in the street to realize that there is no power on earth that can protect him from being bombed. Whatever people may tell him, the bomber will always get through. . . . I just mention that . . . so that people may realize what is waiting for them when the next war comes.

STANLEY BALDWIN, 1932

I do not consider Hitler to be as bad as he is depicted. He is showing an ability that is amazing and he seems to be gaining his victories without much bloodshed.

MAHATMA GANDHI, May 1940

It is significant that despite claims of air enthusiasts no battleship has yet been sunk by bombs.

Caption to a photograph of the U.S.S. *Arizona* in the Army-Navy football game program, November 29, 1941

It is highly unlikely that an airplane, or a fleet of them, could ever sink a fleet of Navy vessels under battle conditions.

FRANKLIN D. ROOSEVELT, 1922

If World War III is fought with atom bombs the war after that will be fought with stones.

ALBERT EINSTEIN

൞ NUCLEAR WAR ൸

The end of the world will be when some enormous boiler shall explode and blow up the globe. And they [the Americans] are great boilermakers.

JULES VERNE

There will one day spring from the brain of science a machine or force so fearful in its potentialities, so absolutely terrifying, that even man, the fighter, who will dare torture and death in order to inflict torture and death, will be appalled, and so abandon war forever. What man's mind can create, man's character can control.

THOMAS ALVA EDISON

We've got to take the atom bomb seriously. It's dynamite.

SAM GOLDWYN

My dynamite will sooner lead to peace than a thousand world conventions. As soon as men will find that in one instant whole armies can be utterly destroyed, they surely will abide by golden peace.

ALFRED BERNHARD NOBEL

The bomb that fell on Hiroshima fell on America, too.

HERMANN HAGEDORN

The atom bomb is a paper tiger with which the Americans try to frighten people.

MAO TSE-TUNG

The atom bomb will never go off, and I speak as an expert on explosives.

ADMIRAL WILLIAM LEAHY, advising President Truman, 1945

Truman did not so much say "yes" as not say "no." It would indeed have taken a lot of nerve to say "no" at that time.

GENERAL LESLIE R. GROVES, on the decision to drop the atomic bomb

No country without an atom bomb could properly consider itself independent.

CHARLES DE GAULLE

The H-bomb rather favors small nations that don't as yet possess it; they feel slightly more free to jostle other nations, having discovered that a country can stick its tongue out quite far these days without provoking war, so horrible are war's consequences.

E. B. WHITE

Nuclear superiority was very useful to us when we had it.

RICHARD M. NIXON

The A-bomb is the most powerful destructive weapon known today. As a believer in humanity I deplore its use, and as a soldier I respect it.

GENERAL OMAR BRADLEY

Nuclear disaster, spread by winds and waters and fear, could well engulf the great and the small, the rich and the poor, the committed and the uncommitted alike. Mankind must put an end to war.

JOHN F. KENNEDY

It is a fundamental law of defense that you always have to use the most powerful weapon you can produce.

MAJOR GENERAL JAMES BURNS

A nation, regardless of its protestations, if it feels that its national existence is threatened and that it is losing a war, will turn to any weapon it can use.

WALTER BEDELL SMITH

Well, boys, I reckon this is it: nuclear combat toe to toe, with the Rooskies!

SLIM PICKENS, as Major T. J. "King" Kong in *Dr. Strangelove or: How I Learned to Stop Worrying and Love the Bomb*

The Bomb brought peace but man alone can keep that peace.

WINSTON CHURCHILL

◈ SCIENCE ◈

War, like most things, is a science to be acquired and perfected by diligence, by perseverance, by time, and by practice.

ALEXANDER HAMILTON

Science is in the saddle. Science is the dictator, whether we like it or not. Science runs ahead of both politics and military affairs. Science evolves new conditions to which institutions must be adapted. Let us keep our science dry.

GENERAL CARL SPAATZ

The influence of the spirit of nationality, that is of democracy, on war is profound, as also were the influences of science and industrial development. The first emotionalized war and, consequently, brutalized it; and the second delivered into the hands of the masses more and more deadly means of destruction.

MAJOR GENERAL J. F. C. FULLER

It is not possession of technology, but its intellectual mastery, which will determine its significance in conflict.

AIR VICE-MARSHAL TONY MASON

Ours is a world of nuclear giants and ethical infants. If we continue to develop our technology without wisdom or prudence, our servant may prove to be our executioner.

GENERAL OMAR BRADLEY

If someone tries to sell you an airplane that can take hits, tell him you want an aircraft that can't take hits.

GENERAL CHARLES HORNER, on the value of stealth aircraft

In the first quarter of the 21st century you will be able to find, fix or track, and target, in near real time, anything of consequence that moves upon or is located on the face of the Earth.

GENERAL RONALD R. FOGLEMAN

So long as we allow tradition, in place of science, to dictate the allocation of our defensive expenditure, we shall dissipate vast sums on pseudo-security, enfeeble our diplomacy and betray the cause of peace.

BRIGADIER GENERAL P. R. C. GROVES

You can't say civilization don't advance . . . for every war they kill you a new way.

WILL ROGERS

❧ MILITARY HISTORY ❧

The most persistent sound which reverberates through men's history is the beating of the war drum.

ARTHUR KOESTLER

War should belong to the tragic past, to history: it should find no place on humanity's agenda for the future.

POPE JOHN PAUL II

History is littered with wars which everybody knew would never happen.

ENOCH POWELL

History teaches that wars begin when governments believe the price of aggression is cheap.

RONALD REAGAN

The whole history of the world is summed up in the fact that, when nations are strong, they are not always just, and when they wish to be just, they are no longer strong.

WINSTON CHURCHILL

War is a matter of vital importance to the State, the province of life and death, the road to survival or ruin. It is therefore mandatory that it be thoroughly studied.

SUN TZU

The military student does not seek to learn from history the minutiae of method and technique. In every age these are influenced by the characteristics of weapons currently available and the means at hand for maneuvering, supplying, and controlling combat forces. But research does bring to light those fundamental principles, and their combinations and applications, which, in the past have produced results.

GENERAL DOUGLAS MACARTHUR

To be a successful soldier you must know history. What you must know is how man reacts. Weapons change but man who uses them changes not at all.

GENERAL GEORGE S. PATTON

It is better to be wise after the event than not wise at all, and wisdom after one event may lead to wisdom before another.

GROUP CAPTAIN JOHN C. SLESSOR

War is not an affair of chance. A great deal of knowledge, study, and meditation is necessary to conduct it well.

FREDERICK THE GREAT

If we only act for ourselves, to neglect the study of history is not prudent; if we are entrusted with the care of others, it is not just.

SAMUEL JOHNSON

Only the study of military history is capable of giving those who have no experience of their own a clear picture of what I have just called the friction of the whole machine.

CARL VON CLAUSEWITZ

Read and re-read the campaigns of Alexander, Hannibal, Caesar, Gustavus Adolphus, Turrene, Eugene, and Frederick. Make them your models. This is the only way to become a great captain and to master the secrets of the art of war.

NAPOLEON BONAPARTE

Only the study of the past can give us a sense of reality and show us how the soldier will fight in the future.

ARDANT DU PICQ, *Battle Studies*

It is in military history that we are to look for the source of all military science. In it we shall find those exemplifications of failure and success by which alone the truth and value of the rules of strategy can be tested.

DENNIS HART MAHAN

It is only possible to probe into the mind of the commander through historical examples.

B. H. LIDDELL HART

Though the military art is essentially a practical one, the opportunities of practicing it are rare. Even the largest scale peace maneuvers are only a feeble shadow of the real thing. So that a soldier desirous of acquiring skill in handling troops is forced to theoretical study of great Captains.

FIELD MARSHAL ARCHIBALD PERCIVAL WAVELL, First Earl Wavell

When it comes to understanding present war conditions and the probable origins of the next war, a deep and impartial knowledge of history is essential.

MAJOR GENERAL J. F. C. FULLER, *Decisive Battles*

Modern warfare has its rules and principles, which it is necessary to thoroughly master before being worthy to command, and it is wiser to profit by such lessons of history, as taught in the work before us than to purchase experience by the blood of battlefields.

LIEUTENANT COLONEL RICHARD TAYLOR

I've been studying the art of war for forty-odd years. When a surgeon decides in the course of an operation to change his objective . . . he is not making a snap decision but one based on knowledge, experience, and training. So am I.

GENERAL GEORGE S. PATTON

Until we understand war in the fullest sense, which involves an understanding of men in war, among other elements, it seems to me that we have no more prospect of preventing war than the savage has of preventing plague.

B. H. LIDDELL HART

The expenses required to prevent a war are much lighter than those that will, if not prevented, be absolutely necessary to maintain it.

BENJAMIN FRANKLIN

Only those to whom the study of war is novel permit themselves to be swept away by novel elements in the present war.

BERNARD BRODIE

Military history, accompanied by sound criticism, is indeed the true school of war.

GENERAL MATTHEW B. RIDGEWAY

❧ EDUCATION ❧

I shall remove from the promotion list any officer whose name I read on the cover of a book.

PATRICE MACMAHON, Marshal of France

The professional military mind is by necessity an inferior and unimaginative mind; no man of high intellectual quality would willingly imprison his gifts in such a calling.

H. G. WELLS

When, in 1898, I joined the Army, though a normally indifferently educated young Englishman, I was appalled by the ignorance which surrounded me and the immense military value attached to it.

MAJOR GENERAL J. F. C. FULLER

No method of education, no system of promotion, no amount of common sense ability is of value unless the leader has in him the root of the matter—the fighting spirit.

FIELD MARSHAL ARCHIBALD PERCIVAL WAVELL, First Earl Wavell

The man who cannot change his mind has become mineralized. He is a walking stone.

MAJOR GENERAL J. F. C. FULLER

For most men, the matter of learning is one of professional preference. But for Army officers, the obligation to learn, to grow in their profession, is clearly a public duty.

GENERAL OMAR BRADLEY

ℛ WAR AIMS ℜ

You ask me for our war aims. My war aim is to be the victor.

GEORGES CLEMENCEAU

Yes, our military will be leaner but the world must know the United States is going to maintain our military superiority with armed forces that are agile, flexible and ready for the full range of contingencies and threats.

BARACK OBAMA

It's not going to look like a win, smell like a win or taste like a win. This is going to end in an argument.

MAJOR GENERAL BILL MAYVILLE, chief of operations for U.S. command in Afghanistan

My message to you today is simple: no matter how much contention and partisanship there appears to be in our country, there is far more that unites us as Americans than divides us.

GENERAL DAVID PETRAEUS

Putting aside all the fancy words and academic doubletalk, the basic reason for having a military is to do two jobs—to kill people and to destroy the works of man.

GENERAL THOMAS S. POWER

There is only one purpose to which a whole society can be directed by a deliberate plan. That purpose is war, and there is no other.

WALTER LIPPMANN

The proper strategy consists in inflicting as telling blows as possible on the enemy's army, and then in causing the inhabitants so much suffering that they must long for peace, and force the government to demand it. The people must be left with nothing but their eyes to weep with after the war.

GENERAL PHILIP H. SHERIDAN

Paralysis, rather than destruction, is the true aim in war, and the most far-reaching in its effects.

B. H. LIDDELL HART

◌ WINNING A WAR ◌

The secret of victory lies not wholly in knowledge. It lurks in that vitalizing spark, intangible yet evident as lightning.

GENERAL GEORGE S. PATTON

The victor will not be asked afterwards whether he told the truth or not.

ADOLF HITLER

When you are winning a war almost everything that happens can be claimed to be right and wise.

WINSTON CHURCHILL

People never lie so much as after a hunt, during a war or before an election.

OTTO VON BISMARCK

One more such victory and we are undone.

PYRRHUS, of Epirus

In war, whichever side may call itself the victor, there are no winners but all are losers.

NEVILLE CHAMBERLAIN

Nothing except a battle lost can be half so melancholy as a battle won.

ARTHUR WELLESLEY, Duke of Wellington

To win, we must have leaders and commanders with fire in their belly.

GENERAL WILLIAM E. DEPUY

Our goal should be to develop leaders who make the difference between winning and losing.

GENERAL CREIGHTON W. ABRAMS

Don't fight a battle if you don't gain anything by winning.

GENERAL GEORGE S. PATTON

What the ancients called a clever fighter is one who not only wins, but excels in winning with ease.

SUN TZU

⚮ VICTORY ⚮

The will to conquer is the first condition of victory.

MARSHAL OF FRANCE FERDINAND FOCH

Too much success is not wholly desirable; an occasional beating is good for men—and nations.

ALFRED THAYER MAHAN

There is nothing certain about war except that one side won't win.

SIR IAN HAMILTON

Victory has a thousand fathers, but defeat is an orphan.

JOHN F. KENNEDY

Who dares, wins.
  Motto of the British Special Air Service regiment

There is no victory except through our imaginations.
  DWIGHT D. EISENHOWER

Any coward can fight a battle when he's sure of winning.
  GEORGE ELLIOT

You ask, what is our aim? I can answer in one word. It is victory. Victory at all costs. Victory in spite of all terrors. Victory, however long and hard the road may be, for without victory there is no survival.
  WINSTON CHURCHILL

Victory is not an end in itself. It is worse than useless if the end of the war finds you so exhausted that you are defeated in the peace. Wise statesmanship must aim at conserving strength so as to be still strong when peace is settled.
  B. H. LIDDELL HART

Only the winners decide what were war crimes.
  GARY WILLS

◈ TERRORISM ◈

There was no silver bullet that could have prevented the 9/11 attacks.

CONDOLEEZZA RICE

Our hearts are broken, but they are beating, and they are beating stronger than ever. We choose to live our lives in freedom.

RUDOLPH W. GIULIANI

This mass terrorism is the new evil in our world today.

TONY BLAIR

Fight terror as if there was no negotiations and conduct the negotiations as if there was no terror.

YITZHAK RABIN

We must recognize the chief characteristic of the modern era—a permanent state of what I call violent peace.

ADMIRAL JAMES D. WATKINS

I'm absolutely convinced that the threat we face now, the idea of a terrorist in the middle of one of our cities with a nuclear weapon, is very real and that we have to use extraordinary measures to deal with it.

DICK CHENEY

As a division commander in Kosovo, I would have said that if I can do conventional war, I can do anything else. Now I know that isn't true.

GENERAL GEORGE CASEY

Because I do it with one small ship, I am called a terrorist. You do it with a whole fleet and are called an emperor.

A pirate, from St. Augustine's *City of God*

If the terrorists are able to get us to change our behavior dramatically so that we are no longer functioning as a free people, then they've won. And we simply can't let that happen.

DONALD RUMSFELD

We must recognize the chief characteristic of the modern era—a permanent state of what I call violent peace.

ADMIRAL JAMES D. WATKINS

Our mission continues . . . The War on Terror continues, yet it is not endless. We do not know the day of final victory, but we have seen the turning of the tide.

GEORGE W. BUSH, in a televised address from the deck of USS *Lincoln*, May 1, 2003. Behind him was the controversial banner "Mission Accomplished" that was put up by the Navy. In January 2009, Bush said that "Clearly, putting 'Mission Accomplished' on an aircraft carrier was a mistake."

I was in Baghdad, and I was given a draft of that thing to look at. And I just died, and I said my God, it's too conclusive. And I fixed it and sent it back . . . they fixed the speech, but not the sign.

DONALD RUMSFELD

❧ VANQUISHED ❧

Conquered people tend to be witty.

SAUL BELLOW

A lost battle is a battle one thinks one has lost.

MARSHAL OF FRANCE FERDINAND FOCH

We have fought this fight as long, and as well as we know how. We have been defeated. For us, as a Christian people, there is now but one course to pursue. We must accept the situation.

GENERAL ROBERT E. LEE

We have resolved to endure the unendurable and suffer what is insufferable.

HIROHITO, Emperor of Japan, after the Hiroshima bombing

There is only one decisive victory: the last.

CARL VON CLAUSEWITZ

In starting and waging a war, it is not fight that matters but victory.

ADOLF HITLER

In war there is no second prize for the runner-up.

GENERAL OMAR BRADLEY

In war there is no substitute for victory.

GENERAL DOUGLAS MACARTHUR

You can no more win a war than you can win an earthquake.

JEANNETTE RANKIN, the first Congresswoman

In war, Resolution; in defeat, Defiance; in victory, Magnanimity; in peace, Goodwill.

WINSTON CHURCHILL

Self-interest as well as humane reasons demand that warring nations should endeavour to gain their end, the moral subjugation of the enemy, with the infliction of the least possible permanent injury to life and industry. For the enemy of to-day is the customer of tomorrow and often the ally of the future.

B. H. LIDDELL HART

◌ DEFEAT ◌

In war the victorious strategist seeks battle after the victory has been won, whereas he who is destined to defeat first fights and afterwards looks to victory.

SUN TZU

Death is nothing, but to live defeated is to die every day.

NAPOLEON BONAPARTE

It was our fault, and our very great fault—now we
must turn it to use.
We have forty million reasons for failure, but not a
single excuse!

RUDYARD KIPLING, "The Lesson"

The general of a large army may be defeated, but you cannot defeat the determined mind of a peasant.

CONFUCIUS

They were never defeated, they were only killed.
Saying about the French Foreign Legion

If you live long enough, you'll see that every victory turns into a defeat.

SIMONE DE BEAUVOIR

Tell General Howard I know his heart. What he told me before in Idaho I have in my heart. I am tired of fighting. My people ask me for food and I have none to give. It is cold and we have no blankets, no wood. My people are starving to death. Where is my little daughter? I do not know. Perhaps even now she is freezing to death. Hear me my chiefs, I have fought. But from where the sun now stands, Joseph will fight no more forever.

CHIEF JOSEPH, of the Nez Percé

◦◦ THE PRESS ◦◦

How is the world ruled and how do wars start? Diplomats tell lies to journalists and then believe what they read.

KARL KRAUS

The printing press is the greatest weapon in the armory of the modern commander.

T. E. LAWRENCE

You furnish the pictures and I'll furnish the war.

WILLIAM RANDOLPH HEARST, in a telegram to Frederic Remington

Four hostile newspapers are more to be feared than a thousand bayonets.

NAPOLEON BONAPARTE

The essence of successful warfare is secrecy. The essence of successful journalism is publicity.

British regulations for War Correspondents, 1960

I am sorry that the movements of the armies cannot keep pace with the expectations of the editors of papers.

GENERAL ROBERT E. LEE

War makes rattling good history; but Peace is poor reading.

THOMAS HARDY

Above all, this book is not concerned with Poetry. The subject of it is War, and the Pity of War. The Poetry is in the pity.

WILFRED OWEN

❧ PROPAGANDA ❧

We must remember that in time of war what is said on the enemy's side of the front is always propaganda and what is said on our side of the front is truth and righteousness, the cause of humanity and a crusade for peace.

WALTER LIPPMANN

It is a very dangerous thing to organize the patriotism of a nation if you are not sincere.

ERNEST HEMINGWAY

Propaganda is a soft weapon: hold it in your hands too long, and it will move about like a snake, and strike the other way.

JEAN ANOUILH

In war, truth is the first casualty.

AESCHYLUS

The leader of genius must have the ability to make different opponents appear as if they belonged to one category.

ADOLF HITLER

It is the merit of a general to impart good news, and to conceal the truth.

SOPHOCLES

Delete any footage which includes the idea that war is not altogether glamorous and noble.

JOSEPH I. BREEN, Hollywood film association executive

We all had to weigh, in the balance, the difference between lives and lies.

COLONEL OLIVER NORTH

War and truth have a fundamental incompatibility. The devotion to secrecy in the interests of the military machine largely explains why, throughout history, its operations commonly appear in retrospect the most uncertain and least efficient of human activities.

B. H. LIDDELL HART

Vietnam was the first war ever fought without any censorship. Without censorship, things can get terribly confused in the public mind.

GENERAL WILLIAM WESTMORELAND

Television brought the brutality of war into the comfort of the living room. Vietnam was lost in the living rooms of America—not on the battlefields of Vietnam.

MARSHALL MCLUHAN

American boys should not be seen dying on the nightly news. Wars should be over in three days or less, or before Congress invokes the War Powers Resolution. Victory must be assured in advance. And the American people must be all for it from the outset.

EVAN THOMAS

❧ POPULARITY OF WARS ❧

As long as war is regarded as wicked, it will always have its fascination. When it is looked upon as vulgar, it will cease to be popular.

OSCAR WILDE

All wars are popular for the first thirty days.

ARTHUR SCHLESINGER, JR.

The troops will march in, the bands will play, the crowds will cheer, and in four days everyone will have forgotten. Then we will be told we have to send in more troops. It's like taking a drink. The effect wears off, and you have to take another.

JOHN F. KENNEDY

Men grow tired of sleep, love, singing and dancing sooner than war.

HOMER

Whenever in our time a war breaks out, there also breaks out, and especially among the most noble members of a people, a secret desire: they throw themselves with delight against the new danger of death, because in the sacrifice for the fatherland they believe they have found at last the permission to evade their human purpose. War is for them a short-cut to suicide, it enables them to commit suicide with a good conscience.

FRIEDRICH NIETZSCHE

❧ MORALE ❧

Morale is the greatest single factor in successful wars.

DWIGHT D. EISENHOWER

In war, morale is to material as three is to one.

NAPOLEON BONAPARTE

Morale: Knowing what you are doing is important, doing it well, knowing it is appreciated.

GENERAL BRUCE C. CLARKE

Morale is a state of mind. It is that intangible force which will move a whole group of men to give their last ounce to achieve something, without counting the cost to themselves.

FIELD MARSHAL SIR WILLIAM J. SLIM

Morale, frankly, is an individual thing. And it often comes down to the kind of day that you're having. I am not immune from those same swings. On days when we have had tough casualties, those are not good days. Morale is not high on those days. And I think the same is true of all of our forces.

GENERAL DAVID PETRAEUS

It is not enough to fight. It is the spirit which we bring to the fight that decides the issue. It is morale that wins the victory.

GENERAL GEORGE MARSHALL

As the war of machines is less destructive to life and property, and more destructive to will and nerves, the tactical object of war will become demoralisation and disorganisation rather than destruction and annihilation.

MAJOR GENERAL J. F. C. FULLER

You really can't blame the military for wanting to go to war [in Iraq]. They've got all these new toys and they want to know whether they work or not.

ANDY ROONEY

The only way the French are going in is if we tell them we found truffles in Iraq.

DENNIS MILLER

The enemy nation's will to resist is subdued by the fact or threat of making life so unpleasant and difficult for the people that they will comply with your terms rather than endure this misery.

B. H. LIDDELL HART

Nothing is worse than that the soldier feels himself neglected in this respect, and to believe himself subject, without his own fault, to an effect to which he is powerless. Defeat would thus appear excusable, and success cannot have a worse enemy than this feeling.

GENERAL KOLMAR VON DER GOLTZ

ᘓ MUSIC AND SOUND ᘔ

Music played at weddings always reminds me of the music played for soldiers before they go into battle.

HEINRICH HEINE

That a man can take pleasure in marching in fours to the strains of a band is enough to make me despise him.

ALBERT EINSTEIN

How good bad music and bad reasons sound when we march against an enemy.

FRIEDRICH NIETZSCHE

Military justice is to justice what military music is to music.

GEORGES CLEMENCEAU

Britain is no longer a world power—all they have left are generals and admirals and bands.

GENERAL GEORGE BROWN

I hated the bangs in the war: I always felt a silent war should have been far more tolerable.

PAMELA HANSFORD JOHNSON

If peace . . . only had the music and pagaentry of war, there'd be no wars.

SOPHIE KERR

For all the great Gaels of Ireland
Are the men that God made mad,
For all their wars are merry,
And all their songs are sad.
G. K. CHESTERTON, *The Ballad of the White Horse*

◌ POLITICIANS ◌

War is "too serious a business" for the destinies of nations to be controlled by mere strategists. There is a need for the wider horizon of grand strategy, which embraces the state of peace that lies beyond every war.
B. H. LIDDELL HART

War is too important to be left to the generals.
GEORGES CLEMENCEAU

The military don't start wars. The politicians start wars.
GENERAL WILLIAM WESTMORELAND

Old men declare war. But it is the youth that must fight and die. And it is youth who must inherit the tribulation, the sorrow, and the triumphs that are the aftermath of war.
HERBERT C. HOOVER

No one man nor group of men incapable of fighting or exempt from fighting should in any way be given the power, no matter how gradually it is given them, to put this country or any country into war.

ERNEST HEMINGWAY

There's no difference between one's killing and making decisions that will send others to kill. It's exactly the same thing, or even worse.

GOLDA MEIR

In our country . . . one class of men makes war and leaves another to fight it out.

GENERAL WILLIAM T. SHERMAN

The British soldier can stand up to anything except the British War Office.

GEORGE BERNARD SHAW

To delight in war is a merit in the soldier, a dangerous quality in the captain and a positive crime in the statesman.

GEORGE SANTAYANA

The politician should fall silent the moment mobilization begins, and not resume his precedence until the strategist has informed the King, after the total defeat of the enemy, that he has completed his task.

FIELD MARSHAL HELMUTH VON MOLTKE THE ELDER

The strategist is he who always keeps the objective of the war in sight and the objective of the war is never military and is always political.

ALFRED THAYER MAHAN

The ultimate object of our wars, the political one, is not always quite a simple one.

CARL VON CLAUSEWITZ

If you are going to kill someone, you better have a good reason for it. And if you have a good reason, then you better not play around with the killing. We didn't seem to have the good reason, and we were playing around with the killing. . . . If I had to be a killer, I wanted to know why I was killing; and the facts didn't match the rhetoric coming out of Washington.

GENERAL CHARLES HORNER, 1999

Political power grows out of the barrel of a gun.

MAO TSE-TUNG

For we had the force, skill, and intelligence, but our civilian betters wouldn't turn us loose.

GENERAL WILLIAM MOMYER

The real tragedy of Vietnam is that this war was not won by the other side, by Hanoi or Moscow or Peiping. It was lost in Washington D.C.

ADMIRAL U. S. GRANT SHARP

The world must be made safe for democracy.

WOODROW WILSON

Threat systems are the basis of politics as exchange systems are the basis of economics.

KENNETH BOULDING

War belongs not to the provinces of Art and Sciences, but to the province of social life. It is a conflict of great interests, which is settled by bloodshed, and only in that is it different from others. It would be better, instead of comparing it with any other Art, to liken it to business competition, which is also a conflict of human interests and activities; and it is still more like State policy, which, again, can be looked on as a kind of business competition on a great scale.

CARL VON CLAUSEWITZ

Nearly all men can stand adversity, but if you want to test a man's character, give him power.

ABRAHAM LINCOLN

A general's dispatch should have more honesty than a politician's electioneering pamphlets.

B. H. LIDDELL HART

Non illegitimi carborundum.
(Don't let the bastards grind you down.)

MOTTO OF GENERAL JOSEPH "VINEGAR JOE" STILWELL

My men and I have decided that our boss, the president of the United States, is as tough as woodpecker lips.

COLONEL CHARLES BECKWITH

⊙ DIPLOMACY ⊙

It is better to have less thunder in the mouth and more lightning in the hand.

GENERAL BEN CHIDLAW

What you do speaks so loud that I cannot hear what you say.

RALPH WALDO EMERSON

The great questions of the day will be decided not by speeches and majority votes . . . but by iron and blood.

OTTO VON BISMARCK

Diplomats are just as essential to starting a war as soldiers are to finishing it. You take Diplomacy out of war and the thing would fall flat in a week.

WILL ROGERS

If we have an arms control agreement, the Russians will cheat. If we have an arms race, we will win.

GENERAL EARLE WHEELER

Speak softly and carry a big stick.

THEODORE ROOSEVELT

Diplomacy is to do and say
The nastiest thing in the nicest way.

ISAAC GOLDBERG

You can get more with a kind word and a gun than you can with a kind word alone.

AL CAPONE

Not believing in force is the same as not believing in gravity.

LEON TROTSKY

An opinion can be argued with; a conviction is best shot.

T. E. LAWRENCE

There is nothing that war has ever achieved we could not better achieve without it.

HAVELOCK ELLIS

Jaw-jaw is better than war-war.

HAROLD MACMILLAN

Diplomacy without armaments is like music without instruments.

FREDERICK THE GREAT

A real diplomat is one who can cut his neighbor's throat without having his neighbor notice it.

TRYGVE LIE

There are a few ironclad rules of diplomacy but to one there is no exception. When an official reports that talks were useful, it can safely be concluded that nothing was accomplished.

JOHN KENNETH GALBRAITH

I'm convinced there's a small room in the attic of the Foreign Office where future diplomats are taught to stammer.

PETER USTINOV

At vast expense the Ambassadors offer up their livers almost every night in the service of their country.

PATRICK O'DONOVAN

The ability to get to the verge without getting into the war is the necessary art. If you try to run away from it, if you are scared to go to the brink, you are lost.

JOHN FOSTER DULLES

A man-of-war is the best ambassador.

OLIVER CROMWELL

Let us never negotiate out of fear. But let us never fear to negotiate.

JOHN F. KENNEDY

More history's made by secret handshakes than by battles, bills, and proclamations.

JOHN BARTH

He lied, I knew he lied and he knew I lied. That was diplomacy.

ADMIRAL WILLIAM KIMBALL

Sincere diplomacy is no more possible than dry water or wooden iron.

JOSEPH STALIN

It is useless to delude ourselves. All the restrictions, all the international agreements made during peacetime are fated to be swept away like dried leaves on the winds of war.

ITALIAN GENERAL GIULIO DOUHET

Treaties are like roses and young girls. They last while they last.

CHARLES DE GAULLE

Negotiation in the classic diplomatic sense assumes parties more anxious to agree than to disagree.

DEAN ACHESON

The principle of give and take is the principle of diplomacy— give one and get ten.

MARK TWAIN

The time has come to stop beating our heads against stone walls under the illusion that we have been appointed police- man to the human race.

WALTER LIPPMANN

It is our true policy to steer clear of permanent alliances with any portion of the foreign world.

GEORGE WASHINGTON

Alliances are held together by fear, not by love.

HAROLD MACMILLAN

If we see that Germany is winning the war we ought to help Russia, and if Russia is winning we ought to help Germany, and in that way let them kill as many as possible.

HARRY S. TRUMAN

Domestic policy can only defeat us; foreign policy can kill us.

JOHN F. KENNEDY

A nation does not have to be cruel to be tough.

FRANKLIN D. ROOSEVELT

Whenever you accept our views we shall be in full agreement with you.

MOSHE DAYAN

There are always three choices—war, surrender, and present policy.

HENRY KISSINGER

The United States never lost a war or won a conference.

WILL ROGERS

❧ COLD WAR ❧

Let us not be deceived—we are today in the midst of a cold war.

BERNARD M. BARUCH

The Superpowers often behave like two heavily armed blind men feeling their way around a room, each believing himself in mortal peril from the other whom he assumes to have perfect vision.

HENRY KISSINGER

We may be likened to two scorpions in a battle, each capable of killing the other, but only at the risk of his own life.

J. ROBERT OPPENHEIMER

We do not want war any more than the West does, but we are less interested in peace than the West, and therein lies the strength of our position.

JOSEPH STALIN

Here's my strategy on the Cold War: We win, they lose.

RONALD REAGAN

✴ ALLIES ✴

We have no eternal allies, and no perpetual enemies. Our interests are eternal and perpetual, and those interests it is our duty to follow.

LORD PALMERSTON

There is at least one thing worse than fighting with allies. And that is to fight without them.

WINSTON CHURCHILL

War without allies is bad enough, with allies it is hell!

MARSHAL OF THE RAF SIR JOHN C. SLESSOR

It is astonishing how obstinate allies are, how parochially minded, how ridiculously sensitive to prestige and how wrapped up in obsolete political ideas. It is equally astonishing how they fail to see how broad-minded you are, how clear your picture is, how up to date you are and how co-operative and big-hearted you are. It is extraordinary.

FIELD MARSHAL SIR WILLIAM J. SLIM

America is the only nation in history which miraculously has gone directly from barbarism to degeneration without the usual interval of civilization.

GEORGES CLEMENCEAU

A nation cannot remain great if it betrays its allies and lets down its friends.

RICHARD M. NIXON

Every nation has to either be with us, or against us. Those who harbor terrorists, or who finance them, are going to pay a price.

HILLARY CLINTON

❧ NATIONALITIES ❧

History tells me that when the Russians come to a country, they don't go back.

MOHAMMED DAOUD, Afghani rebel leader

I cannot forecast to you the action of Russia. It is a riddle wrapped in a mystery inside of an enigma.

WINSTON CHURCHILL

Somebody said the second most stupid thing in the world a man could say was that he could understand the Russians. I've often wondered what in the hell was the first.

RONALD REAGAN

In an English ship, they say, it is poor grub, poor pay, and easy work; in an American ship, good grub, good pay, and hard work. And this is applicable to the working populations of both countries.

JACK LONDON

Nothing unites the English like war. Nothing divides them like Picasso.

HUGH MILLS

They are the scum of the earth. English soldiers are fellows who have enlisted for drink, that is the plain fact; they have all enlisted for drink.

ARTHUR WELLESLEY, Duke of Wellington

It was said in the First World War that the French fought for their country, the British fought for freedom of the seas, and the Americans fought for souvenirs.

HARRY S. TRUMAN

German prisoners, asked to assess their various enemies, have said that the British attacked singing, and the French attacked shouting, but that the Americans attacked in silence. They liked better the men who attacked singing or shouting than the grimly silent men who kept coming on stubbornly without a sound.

JAMES JONES

I hope that on the final settlement of the war, you insist that the Germans retain Lorraine, because I can imagine no greater burden than to be owner of this nasty country where it rains every day and where the whole wealth of the people consists of assorted manure piles.

GENERAL GEORGE S. PATTON

One thing I will say for the Germans, they are always perfectly willing to give somebody else's land to somebody else.

WILL ROGERS

The more we can kill this year, the less will have to be killed the next war, for the more I see of these Indians the more convinced I am that they all have to be killed or maintained as a species of paupers.

GENERAL WILLIAM T. SHERMAN

The Apaches are the most squalid, cowardly, thieving Indians I know, who are making parts of New Mexico like unto the valley of the shadow of death, and I insist that these gorgons of the mountains be hunted to their holes.

MAJOR GENERAL JOHN POPE

ℛ REVOLUTIONS ℛ

Those who make peaceful revolution impossible will make violent revolution inevitable.

JOHN F. KENNEDY

A people that wants to win its independence cannot limit itself to ordinary means of war. Uprisings in mass, revolutionary war, guerrillas everywhere, that is the only means through which a small nation can get the better of a big one, a less strong army be put in a position to resist a stronger and better organized one.

FRIEDRICH ENGELS

A foreign war is a scratch on the arm; a civil war is an ulcer which devours the vitals of a nation.

VICTOR HUGO

Revolutions are not made by fate but by men.

JACOB BRONOWSKI

The Civil War is not ended: I question whether any serious civil war ever does end.

T. S. ELIOT

Revolution is like one cocktail; it just gets you organized for the next.

WILL ROGERS

At least we're getting the kind of experience we need for the next war.

ALLEN DULLES

A revolution is not a bed of roses. A revolution is a struggle to the death between the future and the past.

FIDEL CASTRO

Few revolutionists would be such if they were heirs to a baronetcy.

GEORGE SANTAYANA

Revolutions have never lightened the burden of tyranny, they have only shifted it to another shoulder.

GEORGE BERNARD SHAW

Every revolutionary ends up by becoming either an oppressor or a heretic.

ALBERT CAMUS

If the American Revolution had produced nothing but the Declaration of Independence, it would have been worthwhile.

REAR ADMIRAL SAMUEL ELIOT MORISON

Hate is able to provoke disorders, to ruin a social organization, to cast a country into a period of bloody revolutions; but it produces nothing.

GEORGES SOREL

⊘ GUERRILLA WARFARE ⊘

The guerrilla fights the war of the flea, and his military enemy suffers the dog's disadvantages: too much to defend; too small, ubiquitous and agile an enemy to come to grips with.

ROBERT TABER

A government needs one hundred soldiers for every guerrilla it faces.

FULGENCIO BATISTA

The conventional army loses if it does not win. The guerrilla wins if he does not lose.

HENRY KISSINGER

Subtle and insubstantial, the expert leaves no trace; divinely mysterious, he is inaudible. Thus he is master of his enemy's fate.

SUN TZU

❧ NATIONS FOUNDED ON WAR ❧

A man may build himself a throne of bayonets, but he cannot sit on it.

WILLIAM RALPH INGE

There are no warlike people—just warlike leaders.

RALPH BUNCHE

An empire founded by war has to maintain itself by war.

MONTESQUIEU

All great civilizations, in their early stages, are based on success in war.

SIR KENNETH CLARK

In order to have good soldiers a nation must always be at war.

NAPOLEON BONAPARTE

❧ DETERRENCE ❧

Qui desiderat pacem, praeparet bellum.
(Let him who desires peace, prepare for war.)

VEGETIUS

Forces that cannot win will not deter.

GENERAL NATHAN F. TWINING

Of the four wars in my lifetime none came about because the
United States was too strong.

RONALD REAGAN

Only when our arms are sufficient beyond doubt can we be
certain that they will never be employed.

JOHN F. KENNEDY

I've told you before and I'll tell it to you again. The strong
survive and the weak disappear. We do not propose to disappear.

JIMMY HOFFA

A modern, autonomous, and thoroughly trained Air Force in
being at all times will not alone be sufficient, but without it
there can be no national security.

GENERAL HENRY "HAP" ARNOLD

The longer deterrence succeeds, the more difficult it is to dem-
onstrate what made it work.

HENRY KISSINGER

To be prepared for war is one of the most effectual means of
preserving peace.

GEORGE WASHINGTON

Nations do not arm for war. They arm to keep themselves from war.

SENATOR BARRY GOLDWATER

Men rise from one ambition to another; first they seek to secure themselves from attack, and then they attack others.

NICCOLO MACHIAVELLI

For a people who are free, and who mean to remain so, a well-organized and armed militia is their best security.

THOMAS JEFFERSON

There is no record in history of a nation that ever gained anything valuable by being unable to defend itself.

H. L. MENCKEN

Among other evils which being unarmed brings you, it causes you to be despised.

NICCOLO MACHIAVELLI

Obsolete weapons do not deter.

MARGARET THATCHER

That they may have a little peace, even the best dogs are compelled to snarl occasionally.

WILLIAM FEATHER

In this age when there can be no losers in peace and no victors in war, we must recognize the obligation to match national strength with national restraint.

LYNDON B. JOHNSON

The use or threat of force no longer can or must be an instrument of foreign policy. . . . All of us, and primarily the stronger of us, must exercise self-restraint and totally rule out any outward-oriented use of force.

MIKHAIL GORBACHEV

Our real problem, then, is not our strength today; it is rather the vital necessity of action today to ensure our strength tomorrow.

DWIGHT D. EISENHOWER

No nation ever had an army large enough to guarantee it against attack in time of peace, or ensure it of victory in time of war.

CALVIN COOLIDGE

❧ VIGILANCE ❧

There is no security on this earth; there is only opportunity.

GENERAL DOUGLAS MACARTHUR

We cannot count on the instinct for survival to protect us against war.

RONALD REAGAN

We have tried since the birth of our nation to promote our love of peace by a display of weakness. This course has failed us utterly.

GENERAL GEORGE MARSHALL

Airpower alone does not guarantee America's security, but I believe it best exploits the nation's greatest asset, our technical skill.

GENERAL HOYT S. VANDENBERG

The price of freedom is eternal vigilance.

THOMAS JEFFERSON

Eternal vigilance by the people is the price of liberty.

ANDREW JACKSON

Happy is that city which in times of peace thinks of war.
Inscription in the armory of Venice

One sword keeps another in the sheath.

GEORGE HERBERT

❦ THE ENEMY ❧

We have met the enemy, and they are ours.
COMMODORE OLIVER PERRY

We have met the enemy, and he is us.
WALT KELLY

They were all enemy. They were all to be destroyed.
LIEUTENANT WILLIAM CALLEY, JR.

Can anything be more ridiculous than that a man has a right to kill me because he lives on the other side of the water, and because his ruler has a quarrel with mine, although I have none with him?
BLAISE PASCAL

The art of war is simple enough. Find out where your enemy is. Get at him as soon as you can. Strike at him as hard as you can and as often as you can, and keep moving on.
GENERAL ULYSSES S. GRANT

The object of war is not to die for your country but to make the other bastard die for his.
GENERAL GEORGE S. PATTON

At Victoria Station the R.T.O. [Regional Transport Officer] gave me a travel warrant, a white feather and a picture of Hitler marked "This is your enemy." I searched every compartment but he wasn't on the train.

SPIKE MILLIGAN

The duty of the men at Stalingrad is to be dead.

ADOLF HITLER

No weapon has ever settled a moral problem. It can impose a solution but it cannot guarantee it to be a just one. You can wipe out your opponents. But if you do it unjustly you become eligible for being wiped out yourself.

ERNEST HEMINGWAY

The Nazis are the enemy, Wade into them. Spill their blood. Shoot them in the belly. When you put your hand into a bunch of goo that a moment before was your best friend's face, you'll know what to do.

GEORGE C. SCOTT, in the title role in *Patton*

Cease firing, but if any enemy planes appear, shoot them down in a friendly fashion.

ADMIRAL WILLIAM "BULL" HALSEY, JR.

A prisoner of war is a man who tries to kill you and fails, and then asks you not to kill him.

WINSTON CHURCHILL

ॐ NEUTRALITY ॐ

The principle of neutrality . . . has increasingly become an obsolete conception, and, except under very special circumstances, it is an immoral and shortsighted conception.

JOHN FOSTER DULLES

It is not the neutrals or the lukewarms who make history.

ADOLF HITLER

Neutrals never dominate events. They always sink. Blood alone moves the wheels of history.

BENITO MUSSOLINI

There is such a thing as a man being too proud to fight.

WOODROW WILSON

He who walks in the middle of the road gets hit from both sides.

GEORGE P. SCHULTZ

If a man consults whether he is to fight, when he has the power in his own hands, it is certain that his opinion is against fighting.

LORD HORATIO NELSON

War is an ugly thing, but not the ugliest of things; the decayed and degraded state of moral and patriotic feeling which thinks that nothing is worth war is much worse. A man who has nothing for which he is willing to fight; nothing he cares about more than his personal safety; is a miserable creature who has no chance of being free, unless made and kept so by the exertions of better men than himself.

JOHN STUART MILL

[Peace is] an idea which seems to have originated in Switzerland but has never caught hold in the United States. Supporters of this idea are frequently accused of being unpatriotic and trying to create civil disorder.

DICK GREGORY

Look at the Swiss! They have enjoyed peace for centuries and what have they produced? The cuckoo clock.

ORSON WELLS, as Harry Lime in *The Third Man*

Since it has unhappily proved impossible to safeguard our neutral rights by diplomatic means against the unwarranted infringements they are suffering at the hands of Germany, there may be no recourse but *armed* neutrality.

WOODROW WILSON, January 22, 1917

Dante once said that the hottest places in hell are reserved for those who in a period of moral crisis maintain their neutrality.

JOHN F. KENNEDY

⤜ PEACE ⤛

It isn't enough to talk about peace. One must believe in it. And it isn't enough to believe in it. One must work at it.

ELEANOR ROOSEVELT

Since wars begin in the minds of men, it is in the minds of men that the defenses of peace must be constructed.

Preamble to the Constitution of UNESCO

Peace cannot be kept by force. It can only be achieved by understanding.

ALBERT EINSTEIN

In the art of peace, Man is a bungler.

GEORGE BERNARD SHAW

The mere absence of war is not peace.

JOHN F. KENNEDY

The world will never have a lasting peace so long as men reserve for war the finest human qualities.

JOHN FOSTER DULLES

Long, continuous periods of peace and prosperity have always brought about the physical, mental and moral deterioration of the individual.

BRADLEY A. FISKE

I am not so senseless as to want war. We want peace and understanding, nothing else. We want to give our hand to our former enemies. . . . When has the German people ever broken its word?

ADOLF HITLER

I love peace, and I am anxious that we should give the world still another useful lesson, by showing to them other modes of punishing injuries than by war, which is as much a punishment to the punisher as to the sufferer.

THOMAS JEFFERSON

We will never be able to contribute to building a stable and creative world order until we first form some conception of it.

HENRY KISSINGER

Let us not deceive ourselves; we must elect world peace or world destruction.

BERNARD M. BARUCH

Don't tell me peace has broken out.

BERTOLT BRECHT

He that makes a good war makes a good peace.

GEORGE HERBERT

Those who win a war well can rarely make a good peace and those who could make a good peace would never have won the war.

WINSTON CHURCHILL

I say we are going to have peace even if we have to fight for it.

DWIGHT D. EISENHOWER

"Peace" is when nobody's shooting. A "just peace" is when our side gets what it wants.

BILL MAULDIN

It takes at least two to make peace but only one to make war.

NEVILLE CHAMBERLAIN

When you're at war you think about a better life; when you're at peace you think about a more comfortable one.

THORNTON WILDER

Peace, n. In international affairs, a period of cheating between two periods of fighting.

AMBROSE BIERCE

Peace has her victories No less renowned than war.

JOHN MILTON

If you want peace, understand war.

B. H. LIDDELL HART

Get in a tight spot in combat, and some guy will risk his ass to help you. Get in a tight spot in peacetime, and you go it all alone.

BRENDAN FRANCIS

Peace is not only better than war, but infinitely more arduous.

GEORGE BERNARD SHAW

The most disadvantageous peace is better than the most just war.

ERASMUS

Better to live in peace than to begin a war and lie dead.

CHIEF JOSEPH, of the Nez Percé

There never was a good war, or a bad peace.

BENJAMIN FRANKLIN

Everlasting peace will come to the world when the last man has slain the last but one.

ADOLF HITLER

It is the greatest possible mistake to mix up disarmament with peace. When you have peace you will have disarmament.

WINSTON CHURCHILL

The soldier, having experience of war, fears it far more than the doctrinaire who, being ignorant of war, talks only of peace.

GENERAL HANS VON SEECKT

War will never be abolished by people who are ignorant of war.

WALTER LIPPMANN

To put it bluntly, mushy descriptions of peace operations as humanitarian, and neutral efforts to promote peace, stability, and motherhood don't go far enough to explain why so many soldiers die in them or why they so strain the resources of intervening states.

COLONEL ROBERT C. OWEN

Was peace maintained by the risk of war, or because the adversary never intended aggression in the first place?

HENRY KISSINGER

Mark! where his carnage and his conquests cease!
He makes a solitude, and calls it—peace!

LORD BYRON

Five great enemies to peace inhabit with us—avarice, ambition, envy, anger, and pride. If those enemies were to be banished, we would infallibly enjoy perpetual peace.

PETRARCH

Just as war is freedom's cost, disagreement is freedom's privilege.

BILL CLINTON

They make a desert and call it peace.

CORNELIUS TACITUS, Roman historian

⟐ PACIFICISM ⟐

True pacifism is the finest form of manliness. But if a man comes up to you and cuts your hand off, you don't offer him the other one. Not if you want to go on playing the piano, you don't.

SAM PECKINPAUGH

We have met here to fight against war. The truth is that one may not and should not in any circumstances or under any pretext kill his fellow man.

LEO TOLSTOY

My pacifism is not based on any intellectual theory but on a deep antipathy to every form of cruelty and hatred.

ALBERT EINSTEIN

There are only two classes who, as categories, show courage in war—the front-line soldier and the conscientious objector.

B. H. LIDDELL HART

The pacifist is as surely a traitor to his country and to humanity as is the most brutal wrongdoer.

THEODORE ROOSEVELT

Pacifism is simply undisguised cowardice.

ADOLF HITLER

War hath no fury like a non-combatant.

C. E. MONTAGUE

Those who do not go to war roar like lions.

KURDISH PROVERB

Sometime they'll give a war and nobody will come.

CARL SANDBURG

I discovered to my amazement that average men and women were delighted at the prospect of war. I had fondly imagined what most pacifists contended, that wars were forced upon a reluctant population by despotic and Machiavellian governments.

BERTRAND RUSSELL

I have always been against the pacifists during the war, and against the jingoists at the end.

WINSTON CHURCHILL

A bayonet is a weapon with a worker at both ends.
    British pacifist slogan

As long as armies exist, any serious conflict will lead to war.
A pacifism which does not actively fight against the armament
of nations is and must remain impotent.

ALBERT EINSTEIN

⚮ GOD ⚮

The Lord is a man of war.
    Exodus 15:3

War is a necessary part of God's arrangement of the world. . . .
Without war, the world would slide dissolutely into material-
ism.

FIELD MARSHAL HELMUTH VON MOLTKE THE ELDER

Every man thinks God is on his side.

JEAN ANOUILH

You're basically killing each other to see who's got the better
imaginary friend.

YASSER ARAFAT, on going to war over religion

What mean and cruel things men do for the love of God.

W. SOMERSET MAUGHAM

All the gods are dead except the god of war.

ELDRIDGE CLEAVER

God is always on the side of the big battalions.

MARSHAL HENRI DE LA TOUR D'AUVERGNE, Vicomte de Turenne

Oho, the Pope! How many battalions does he have?

JOSEPH STALIN

There are no atheists in fox holes.

WILLIAM THOMAS CUMMINGS, also attributed to Ernie Pyle

⊗ MORALITY OF WAR ⊗

There should be nothing agreeable about warfare. God forbid that I should recommend brutality, but we face facts like men. It is not a trade for a philosopher.

CLAUDE LAMORAL II, Prince de Ligne of Austria

If we must be enemies, let us be men, and fight it out as we propose to do, and not deal in hypocritical appeals to God and humanity.

GENERAL WILLIAM T. SHERMAN, to General John Bell Hood, outside Atlanta, 1864

It is a perplexing and pleasant truth that when men already have something worth fighting for, they do not feel like fighting.

ERIC HOFFER

Truth alone is but a weak motive of action with men, and hence there is always a great difference between knowing and action, between science and art.

CARL VON CLAUSEWITZ

To fight for a reason and in a calculating spirit is something your true warrior despises.

GEORGE SANTAYANA

If man is not ready to risk his life, where is his dignity?

ANDRÉ MALRAUX

◎ DEATH AND DYING ◎

The tyrant dies and his rule is over; the martyr dies and his rule begins.

SØREN KIERKEGAARD

If the war didn't happen to kill you it was bound to start you thinking.

GEORGE ORWELL

I only wish during the war they'd a took me in the army. I coulda been dead by now.

ARTHUR MILLER

When it comes to dying for your country, it's better not to die at all.

LEW AYRES, as Paul Baumer in *All Quiet on the Western Front*

Patriots always talk of dying for their country and never of killing for their country.

BERTRAND RUSSELL

They died to save their country and they only saved the world.

HILAIRE BELLOC

Whenever you hear a man speak of his love for his country it is a sign that he expects to be paid for it.

H. L. MENCKEN

It has been argued that, when killing is viewed as not only permissible but heroic behavior sanctioned by one's government or cause, the fine distinction between taking a human life and other forms of impermissible violence gets lost, and rape becomes an unfortunate but inevitable by-product of the necessary game called war.

SUSAN BROWNMILLER

Sometimes the worst thing we can know about a man is that he has survived. Those who say that life is worth living at any cost have already written for themselves an epitaph of infamy, for there is no cause and no person they will not betray to stay alive.

SIDNEY HOOK

... there are few that die well in a battle; for how can they charitably dispose of any thing when blood is their argument?

WILLIAM SHAKESPEARE

The men that war does not kill it leaves completely transparent.

BRAZILIAN COLONEL CASTELO BRANCO

The question so often asked, "Would the survivors envy the dead?" may turn out to have a simple answer. No, they would be incapable of such feelings. They would not so much envy as, inwardly and outwardly, resemble the dead.

ROBERT JAY LIFTON

It takes twenty years or more of peace to make a man; it takes only twenty seconds of war to destroy him.

KING BAUDOUIN I, of Belgium

Wars, conflict, it's all business. One murder makes a villain. Millions a hero. Numbers sanctify.

CHARLIE CHAPLIN, in the title role of *Monsieur Verdoux*

What are the lives of a million men to me!

NAPOLEON BONAPARTE

A single death is a tragedy, a million deaths is a statistic.

JOSEPH STALIN

Death has a tendency to encourage a depressing view of war.

DONALD RUMSFELD

The graveyards are full of indispensable men.

CHARLES DE GAULLE

War would end if the dead could return.

STANLEY BALDWIN

Only the dead have seen the end of war.

PLATO

If I should die, think only this of me:
That there's some corner of a foreign field
That is for ever England. There shall be
In that rich earth a richer dust concealed;
A dust whom England bore, shaped, made aware,
Gave, once, her flowers to love, her ways to roam,
A body of England's, breathing English air,
Washed by the rivers, blest by the suns of home.

RUPERT BROOKE, "The Soldier." Brooke died in 1915
aboard a French hospital ship bound for Galipoli and
is buried on the Greek island of Skyros.

Put out that damn cigarette.

> H. H. MUNRO (SAKI), last words before being hit with a sniper's bullet, November 14, 1916

Strike the tent.

> GENERAL ROBERT E. LEE, last words

ℰ INDEX ℐ